Second helpings

FURTHER IRISH ADVENTURES WITH FOOD

For Máire – who else would put up with me?

Second Helpings

FURTHER IRISH ADVENTURES WITH FOOD

PAUL FLYNN

THE TANNERY RESTAURANT

WITH CARTOONS BY **KEN BUGGY**
& PHOTOGRAPHY BY **EILEEN HYLAND**

The Collins Press

First published in 2005 by
The Collins Press,
West Link Park,
Doughcloyne,
Wilton,
Cork

A CIP catalogue record of this book is available from the British Library.

Flynn, Paul, 1965-
Second Helpings
1. Cookery
I. Title II. Buggy, Ken
641.5
ISBN 1903464846

Design and typesetting: Stuart Coughlan @ edit+

Printed in Malta

FURTHER IRISH ADVENTURES WITH FOOD

CONTENTS

INTRODUCTION

I am an obsessive collector of cookery books. My ever-expanding book shelves groan under the weight of the various publications: large, forbidding tomes and light frivolous ones. I love them all. I am forever being chastised by my wife for buying them and never really reading them. I ooh and aah at the particular dishes that take my fancy but protest that one day I will get the time. She, however, is the one who truly absorbs them, taking them to bed night after night. When I wonder about a particular partner for an ingredient she might inform me with authority that Bill Granger did such and such with chicken in *Bill's Open Kitchen*, or that Bruno Loubet's cod in *Bistro Bruno* is fantastic.

I flick through these books and derive comfort and inspiration from them. As a chef / proprietor, everyone looks to you for inspiration but sometimes I would like to have my own wise man on a mountain who dispensed advice, Karate Kid-style – 'oyster with cider might be nice – grasshopper!'

Cooking is such a mighty craft. I certainly have done OK practising my technique and my style of food but there is always so much more to learn. This is why I treasure my collection. It is wisdom I wouldn't ordinarily have access to. With this, my second book, I have written the book I always wanted to write. It has been a bit of a struggle, I admit, fitting the writing into my day's work, and sometimes it seemed it would never be finished. Without Orla Broderick's help and guidance I might still be writing. Ken Buggy's cartoons are an integral part of the book, placing my tongue firmly in my cheek as regards to everything except the food. Ken, from Buggy's Glencairn Inn in west Waterford, is a great cook and restaurateur with a

delightfully eccentric view on life. He is, to my knowledge, the only publican to admonish his punters for drinking too much and not give a hoot about the consequences. I have always loved his quirky illustrations and I hope you do too.

This book, to me, represents all my 'uncheffy' ambitions, with relatively simple food that's 'do-able' at home and hopefully you will have a laugh as well. It features me me me in all my self-deprecating glory.

I wanted to write and formulate recipes the way I do every week in the kitchen – devising dishes according to what is available to us. I let this and the weather dictate how I structure a dish: cream and root vegetables in the depth of winter; olive oil and tomatoes for the summer months. The book is therefore divided into sections, with starters, main courses and desserts given for each month. The emphasis is on ease of preparation for the keen home cook.

Cooking is all about mood and feeling. I would like to think that *Second Helpings* will offer you some source of inspiration in the kitchen.

When checking a table in the restaurant one evening, my wife noticed one lady had not touched her scallops. My wife asked if everything was OK and the lady replied, 'Oh, fine. It's just that I only eats chicken'. Go figure. So, grammar aside, there are some situations where there are no answers. All in a day's work ...

*Last year we realised a lifelong ambition
and visited Australia.*

JANUARY

I look forward to January. I don't mind the cold, the wind and incessant rain, since the second week of January we close the restaurant for two and a half weeks and we go on holidays, more often than not to sunnier climes. Like every normal human being I look forward to my holidays and after a busy Christmas I need the rest. I concentrate on being on the other side of the restaurant fence, being looked after and fed as opposed to the other way around.

At this time of year our customers are fed up of eating and are financially drained from the demands of their little Harrys and Sophies, and their need to possess all the consumer goods in the world before they are six. Our holidays are always, one way or another, busman's holidays. You may pooh-pooh this, thinking I need to get a life and you may be right, but nothing makes me happier than eating and being amidst good food.

Last year we realised a lifelong ambition and visited Australia. The Victoria and Prahan markets in Melbourne made me sizzle with excitement. I'm not lying when I tell you that a bevy of page 3 babes might have to wait for me patiently while I perused the market before I get to them – Oh God, I must be getting old.

The fantastic St Jame's market in Brisbane is a stunning symbol of successful urban renewal and community life. Ah, then there's the restaurants: ECCO in Brisbane, Botanical in Melbourne and the incomparable, indisputable king, Neil Perry's Rockpool in Sydney. A truly great restaurant that is simple and unpretentious, yet as polished as your grannie's door knob before a *Corpus Christie* procession.

For me, Australia is the new Mecca. Even simple cafés have an easy style, and a casual inventiveness and unwillingness to settle for anything but quality. I will return – someday.

WHAT'S IN SEASON IN JANUARY

FRUIT cooking apples, pears and forced rhubarb **VEGETABLES** artichokes (Jerusalem), beetroot, Brussels sprouts, cabbages (green, red, Savoy and white), carrots, celeriac, chard, chicory, curly kale, leeks, mushrooms, onions, parsnips, potatoes, salsify, sea kale, shallots, spring onions, spring greens, swede and turnip **FISH** cod, black sole, grey mullet, haddock, halibut, lemon sole, lobster, oysters, red mullet, scallops and turbot **POULTRY** goose, guinea fowl and turkey **MEAT** beef, pork and hogget **GAME** hare, pheasant, pigeon, rabbit, snipe and venison.

ROASTED FiELD MUSHROOM SOUP WiTH CASHEL BLUE AND PiNE NUTS

I just love this soup. Flat cap or field mushrooms, call them what you like, are packed with flavour and I think even better if you use seconds. You'll get them cheap from your veg man after 2 or 3 days. Around this time, their flavour seems to mature and become more intense. It's important never to wash mushrooms as they just absorb the water through their pores. It's best to wipe them with a damp cloth or brush and, although tedious, the result is worthwhile.

Serves 4 as a starter or light lunch

1 tablespoon raisins
4 large flat cap mushrooms, cleaned (with a generous cup)
4 tablespoons olive oil, plus extra for greasing
1 large garlic clove, finely chopped
good pinch chopped fresh thyme
pinch pine nuts
good knob butter
large slice Cashel blue cheese (about 100 g / 4 oz)
300 ml / 1/2 pint bottle Cidona (dry cider)
300 ml / 1/2 pint cream
100 ml / 31/2 fl oz milk
salt and freshly ground black pepper

Preheat the oven to 200°C/400°F/Gas 6. Soak the raisins in a small bowl of boiling water for 20 minutes to plump up, then drain well. Place the mushrooms in a lightly oiled deep roasting tin, skin side down. Divide the raisins, garlic, thyme and pine nuts among them. Season to taste and dot over the butter and Cashel blue, then drizzle a tablespoon of the olive oil over each one. Cover with tin foil and roast for 15 minutes, then remove the foil and cook for another 5 minutes until completely tender and golden brown.

Transfer the roasted mushrooms to deep ovenproof serving bowls and keep warm. Place the roasting tin directly on the hob and pour the Cidona over. Bring to the boil, scraping the bottom of the tin with a wooden spatula to remove any sediment, and then continue to boil fast until reduced by half, stirring occasionally. Pour in the cream and milk and bring to a simmer, then season to taste and ladle around the roasted mushrooms to serve.

If a field mushroom were a fellow, he would be strictly butch and macho to the hilt. His buddies would be the Béarnaise and red wine sauces of this world and Machiavellian garlic would be a cautiously close friend. He would socialise with white truffle oil for that special night out but always mix with that rough and ready trio, bacon, egg and sausage. He would dress in crisp herby breadcrumbs to meet rocket and her ever-present friend Parmesan or just be supportive to chicken, beef or cod. I am really jealous – everyone likes this guy.

CREAMED SALT COD WITH CRISPY BLACK PUDDING AND PARSLEY OIL

I haven't added salt and pepper to this dish as the cod, if salted, has enough and black puddings normally have enough black pepper. The creamed salt cod makes an excellent dip and is wonderful served warm or cold. If you don't fancy it or find it difficult to get hold of use skinless and boneless fresh cod instead. Chopped fresh parsley makes a good substitute for the parsley oil if you haven't had time to make your own.

Serves 4 as a starter or light lunch

200 ml / 7 fl oz milk
1 bay leaf
1 small onion, sliced
150 g / 5 oz salt cod, soaked overnight
2 egg yolks
1 large garlic clove, peeled
100 ml / 3^1/$_2$ fl oz vegetable oil, plus a little extra if necessary
50 ml / 2 fl oz extra virgin olive oil
1 small black pudding, peeled and sliced into 1 cm / ^{1}/$_2$ in rounds

For the Parsley Oil

handful fresh flat-leaf parsley leaves
50 ml / 2 fl oz olive oil
50 ml / 2 fl oz sunflower oil
juice of ^{1}/$_2$ lemon
salt and freshly ground black pepper

To make the parsley oil, place the parsley in a bowl with the olive oil, sunflower oil and lemon juice. Whiz with a hand blender until smooth, then season to taste. Transfer to a sterilised screw-topped jar and store in the fridge until needed – it will keep for up to 2 weeks, then use as required.

Place the milk in a small pan with the bay leaf and onion, then bring to a gentle simmer. Add the soaked salt cod and allow it to poach for 3-4 minutes until just cooked through. Remove from the heat and drain away the liquid. Leave to cool a little, then flake the salt cod, discarding the skin and any bones. Throw away the bay leaf but reserve the onion.

Put the egg yolks in a food processor or liquidiser with the garlic and two tablespoons of water. Blitz until the egg yolks have turned white, then add the flaked cod and reserved onion and continue to blend until you have achieved a smooth paste. With the motor still running, drizzle in the vegetable and olive oil until you get a smooth creamy texture. If it is too stiff add a little more water or if it is too wet add some more vegetable oil. The consistency should be like light whipped cream.

Preheat a grill and arrange the black pudding on the grill rack. Cook for 1-2 minutes on each side until cooked through and sizzling. Spoon the creamed salt cod on to warmed serving plates and arrange the black pudding slices on top. Drizzle the parsley oil on top to serve.

ED HICK'S SAUSAGES WITH CARAMELISED ONIONS AND MAPLE SYRUP

Ed Hick makes the finest sausages in Ireland. Whether you have the venison, chorizo, lamb, Cumberland or any of his other wonderful creations you won't find better. Paired with silky mashed potato and these Boston baked beans, it's the ultimate comfort food.

Serves 4

a little vegetable oil
8 sausages (preferably Hick's)
knob butter
2 onions, thinly sliced
400 g / 14 oz can butter beans, drained and rinsed
1 tablespoon Demerara sugar
1 teaspoon dry mustard powder
1 tablespoon treacle
200 ml / 7 fl oz chicken stock
2 ripe pears, peeled, quartered and cored
drizzle maple syrup
2 tablespoons chopped fresh flat-leaf parsley
salt and freshly ground black pepper
mashed potato, to serve

Preheat the oven to 180°C/350°F/Gas 4. Heat a large ovenproof frying pan or roasting tin directly on the hob. Add the oil and then fry the sausages for about 10 minutes, turning regularly until lightly golden all over. Transfer to a plate.

Reduce the heat of the pan and add the butter. Tip in the onions and sauté for 3-4 minutes until light golden brown, then stir in the beans, sugar, mustard, treacle and stock. Bring to a simmer, stirring, and season to taste. Arrange the sausages on top with the pear quarters and drizzle over a little maple syrup.

Transfer the pan to the oven to bake for 15 minutes until the sausages are completely cooked through and the pears and beans are tender. Scatter over the parsley and arrange on warmed serving plates with the mash to serve.

ROAST CATALAN CHICKEN

Joseph is a Catalan chef that left us last September after 18 months. Quite simply he was one of the best cooks I have ever come across, not in a cheffy way – there were no tottering towers or fancy sugar work to his cooking – just deep, true, beautiful flavours. He cooked like I imagine one of those mythical cherished grandmothers cooked, coaxing out every inch of flavour from simple ingredients. He invariably was railroaded into making staff lunch almost every day because otherwise it was Donegal Catch and chips or some sort of leftover surprise. Dodgy kebabs were dropped in favour of chorizo and fried egg sandwiches dripping with aïoli and chorizo oil. Just the thing to satisfy all and sundry after a hard day with a few well-earned beers. We all miss him. This dish was cooked for staff one day and subsequently featured on our early bird menu on a regular basis, as it can be taken as far as the final baking stage earlier in the day.

Serves 4 – 6

good splash olive oil
2 large onions, finely chopped
5 garlic cloves, finely chopped
1 large chicken, jointed into 8 pieces
handful hazelnuts or almonds
1 tablespoon plain flour
good pinch chopped fresh rosemary and thyme
$1/2$ bottle white wine
375 ml / 13 fl oz chicken stock
4 large potatoes, cut into 2 cm / $3/4$ in cubes
handful ready-to-eat prunes, roughly chopped
salt and freshly ground black pepper
buttery Brussels sprouts, to serve

Preheat the oven to 200°C / 400°F / Gas 6. Heat a little of the olive oil in a heavy-based pan and add the onions. Cook on the lowest heat possible for 2 hours, stirring occasionally until they have caramelised and are a deep brown colour. Stir in the garlic and cook for another 10 minutes, stirring occasionally.

Meanwhile, arrange the chicken pieces in a roasting tin and season all over, then drizzle with a little of the olive oil and roast for 20 minutes until lightly golden but not quite cooked through.

Place the hazelnuts or almonds on a baking sheet and roast for 4-5 minutes until golden brown. Leave to cool a little and then rub off the skins before finely chopping.

Stir the flour into the caramelised onions with the hazelnuts or almonds and herbs, then cook for 2-3 minutes, stirring constantly to ensure that the flour doesn't catch on the bottom of the pan. Gradually stir the wine and stock, making sure that the sauce is smooth after each addition. Simmer over a gentle heat for 15 minutes until slightly reduced and thickened, stirring occasionally. Season to taste.

Remove the chicken pieces from the oven and add the potatoes, tossing so they become well coated in the juices. Return to the oven for another 10 minutes, then scatter over the prunes and pour over the caramelised onion sauce. Bake for another 10-15 minutes until the chicken and potatoes are cooked through and tender. Divide among warmed serving plates and serve at once with a bowl of buttery Brussels sprouts.

I don't mind telling you that I have occasionally pictured a dish in my head as a definite success, but it can look a complete dog's dinner on the plate.

SEARED SCALLOPS WITH SWEET AND SOUR CABBAGE AND CRISPY GARLIC

Scallops are truly special when married with Chinese flavours – ginger, garlic and chilli. This trilogy reminds me of the first time I ever tasted scallops Chinese style in Mr Kong, Lilse Street, Soho, back when I was only a puppy. They were steamed in their shells with just a little of each of the above and anointed with soy sauce, a death row meal if there ever was one. Cabbage lends itself surprisingly well to fish, particularly scallops. One of the first dishes I ever remember seeing in Chez Nico, the eponymous restaurant in which I trained, was seared scallops nestled in a delicate tomato sauce surrounding a bright green mound of buttery cabbage. Simple yet good enough to be served in a two Michelin starred restaurant. This also makes a great starter if you prefer; just reduce the amount of scallops and cabbage and, of course, there's no need for the noodles or rice.

Serves 4

splash olive oil
20 scallops, cleaned and trimmed (with or without roe, whatever takes your fancy)
small knob butter
2 large garlic cloves, thinly sliced
1/2 lime, pips removed

For the Sweet and Sour Cabbage

350 g / 12 oz cabbage, thick stalks removed and very finely shredded
large pinch of salt
splash toasted sesame oil
1 small red chilli, sliced (you can use less if you don't like it too hot)
knob fresh root ginger, peeled and finely diced
25 ml / 1 fl oz white wine vinegar
25 g / 1 oz raisins
25 g / 1 oz pickled ginger, sliced (optional)
1/2 teaspoon sifted icing sugar
salt and freshly ground black pepper
noodles tossed with soy sauce and shredded spring onions, or boiled rice with soy sauce for dipping

To make the cabbage dish, place the cabbage in a large bowl and sprinkle with the salt. Turn lightly to coat and leave for 2 hours. This will take the excess liquid from the cabbage and result in a crisper texture. Rinse well under cold water and pat dry.

Heat the sesame oil in a wok or large frying pan. Tip in the chilli and ginger and quickly fry for about 20 seconds. Toss in the cabbage and fry for another 1–2 minutes. Add the vinegar, raisins and pickled ginger, if using, and fry for 1 minute. Then add the icing sugar and allow to dissolve so the cabbage slightly caramelises. This should take no more than 1–2 minutes. Season to taste and keep warm.

To prepare the scallops heat the olive oil in a heavy-based or non-stick frying pan until smoking hot. Season the scallops and place them carefully in the pan. Cook for 1 1/2 minutes on one side, then turn over and add the butter and garlic. Cook for another minute until tender. Remove the pan from the heat and squeeze the lime juice over. Remove the scallops and garlic from the pan with a slotted spoon and drain on some kitchen paper.

Place the sweet and sour cabbage in the centre of warmed serving plates and arrange the scallops around the edges with the garlic. Serve at once with the noodles or rice and dishes of soy sauce for dipping.

RED MULLET AND CHICKPEA STEW WITH TOMATO AND CUMIN

I'm a big fan of red mullet. It's huge on the continent, fetching prices that compare with those of turbot and sea bass. We in Ireland, however, underrate it. I think we subconsciously liken it to grey mullet. The red mullet though is a fine fish, but one that suffers from very bad press. That's perhaps its own fault for hanging around in shallow waters that are less than pristine. Grey mullet, caught in deeper waters, are as good as any fish you are likely to taste and best of all they are cheap. But back to the red fellow; its glistening skin and white meaty, distinctive flesh pair wonderfully with tomatoes and cumin. In the depths of January, when there is little in the way of seasonal fruit and veg, I have no shame in admitting that I cast an eye over whatever good canned ingredients are available and this is a prime example. I usually cook my own chickpeas but the canned variety are perfectly good; canned tomatoes are the only ones worth using in January but some are better than others and the cumin lends a fabulous musty warmth to the dish. I'm recommending to serve this dish with some spaghettini turned in orange saffron cream but if you don't fancy making this then your favourite pasta, turned in a little butter, salt and pepper will do, as will some plain boiled rice.

Serves 4

1 tablespoon cumin seeds

knob butter

splash olive oil

1 large onion, finely diced

2 celery sticks, finely diced

2 large garlic cloves, crushed

1 glass white wine

400 g /14 oz can tomatoes, whized roughly with a hand blender

squeeze tomato purée

pinch finely chopped fresh rosemary

1 glass chicken stock

pinch sugar

2 x 400 g / 14 oz cans chickpeas, drained and rinsed (or use 400 g / 14 oz home-cooked – see recipe intro.)

8 red mullet fillets, pin bones removed

a little seasoned flour

225 g / 8 oz spaghettini

For the Saffron Cream

pinch saffron strands

juice of 1 orange

1 teaspoon Dijon mustard

150 ml / 1/4 pint cream

salt and freshly ground black pepper

fresh bay leaves to garnish

To make the saffron cream, place the saffron in a heatproof bowl and pour over enough boiling water to just barely cover it. Allow to sit for 10 minutes, then add the orange juice, mustard and seasoning and whisk well with a fork, taking care to leave all the saffron in the bowl and not on the fork. Add the cream and mix until well combined. Cover with cling film and chill for no less than 1 hour or up to 3 days is fine.

Roast the cumin seeds in a dry pan over a medium heat for 2-3 minutes. Remove from the heat and pound in a pestle and mortar or crush on a board with the base of a pan or rolling pin.

Melt the butter with most of the olive oil in a pan and add the onion and celery, then cook for 10 minutes over a low heat. Add the garlic and cumin and cook for 1 minute, then add the white wine. Reduce by half, then add the tomatoes, tomato purée, rosemary, chicken stock and sugar. Cook slowly for 10-15 minutes, the longer and slower the better, stirring occasionally. Add the chickpeas and season to taste.

Take a non-stick frying pan and add the remainder of the oil. Dust the red mullet fillets in the seasoned flour, shaking off any excess. When the pan is smoking, add the fish, skin side down, and cook for 1 minute over a high heat. Turn over, take off the heat and leave to rest in the pan – if your pan isn't big enough you'll need to do this in two batches.

Meanwhile, plunge the spaghettini into a large pan of boiling salted water and cook for 6-8 minutes or according to packet instructions until *al dente* – just tender to the bite. When you are about to use the saffron cream give it a stir. Drain the pasta and add the saffron cream, stirring until heated through, then tip into a warmed serving bowl Spoon the chickpea and tomato sauce on to a warmed seving plate and arrange the red mullet fillets on top to serve. Garnish with the bay leaves.

TIP

Saffron cream goes with any fish – just drizzle a little on top of grilled fish or lobster.

POACHED WINTER FRUITS WITH POWER'S WHISKEY & VANILLA CREAMED RICE

Poached dried fruits are a real favourite of mine. Use what you like, plums, apples, apricots or a mixture of all three like I do for colour and variety. The rice is essentially a chilled rice pudding but without that tackiness you often get. I use Powers whiskey, but you can substitute any other or try using brandy. These fruits keep forever covered in a jar in the fridge so double up the recipe to save you a job down the line.

Serves 4

250 g / 9 oz caster sugar
pared rind $1/2$ orange
1 cinnamon stick
1 Earl Grey tea bag
275 g / 10 oz ready-to-eat mixed dried fruit, such as plums, apples and apricots
good splash Powers whiskey

For the Vanilla Creamed Rice

50 g / 2 oz butter
125 g / $4^1/2$ oz short-grain or Arborio rice (risotto)
1 vanilla pod, halved lengthways and seeds scraped out or 2 drops vanilla extract
500 ml / 16 fl oz milk
500 ml / 16 fl oz cream
icing sugar, to dust (optional)

TIP

This would also be delicious served with some toasted almonds.

Preheat the oven to 160°C/325°F/Gas 3. To make the vanilla creamed rice, melt the butter in a heavy-based pan over a low heat, then tip in the rice and cook for 5 minutes, stirring continuously. Stir in the vanilla with the milk and cream and bring to the boil. Remove from the heat and transfer to a deep ovenproof dish, then cover with foil. Bake for 45 minutes to 1 hour, stirring every 20 minutes until the rice is soft and creamy. The mixture will appear quite runny but the rice will reabsorb this as it cools. Stir occasionally while cooling to make sure that no lumps form. Chill for at least 4 hours before serving.

To make the poaching liquid, place 450 ml/ $3/4$ pint of water in a pan with the sugar, orange rind and cinnamon, then bring to the boil. Drop in the tea bag and simmer for another minute. Remove the tea bag and tip in the dried fruit. Cook very gently for 15 minutes, then stir in the whiskey. Cook for another 2-3 minutes, then remove from the heat and allow the fruit to cool in the liquid.

To serve, divide the poached fruit among serving bowls with some of the flavoured syrup. Place generous spoonfuls of the vanilla creamed rice on top. Dust with icing sugar if you like.

I remember being thirteen and leaning out of my bedroom window praying for a naked woman to appear. Lord only knows what I would do with her if she ever turned up. Nevertheless, this carry on lasted almost a week, only to be stopped by an acute chest cold.

COFFEE AND CHOCOLATE ECLAIRS

Who doesn't love eclairs? I was once in a competition to see who could eat the most eclairs – guess who won? I'm not telling you how many I managed but let's just say people were quite impressed. I serve these to customers but I always manage to scoff one or two myself. Us cooks need a treat after a hard day's toil.

Serves 6 – 8

250 ml / 9 fl oz milk or water, or a mixture of both
pinch salt
2 tablespoons caster sugar
65 g / 2^1/$_2$ oz butter, cut in small pieces
125 g / 4^1/$_2$ oz plain flour
4 eggs
grapeseed or sunflower oil, for greasing
3 tablespoons ground coffee diluted with a little hot water or 2 tablespoons coffee extract
350 g / 12 oz icing sugar
300 ml / ^{1}/$_2$ pint cream
100 g / 4 oz plain chocolate, grated (at least 55 per cent cocoa solids)
^{1}/$_2$ vanilla pod, split in half lengthways and scraped out or 1 drop vanilla extract

Preheat the oven to 180˚C / 350˚F / Gas 4. Place the milk or water, or a mixture of both, in a pan with the salt, caster sugar, and butter. Bring to the boil over a gentle heat. As the mixture starts to boil, take off the heat and tip in all the flour, mixing quickly to combine. Return the pan to the heat and thicken the paste, stirring continuously with a wooden spoon. It takes about 1 minute for the pastry to leave the sides of the pan. When this happens, remove the pan from the heat and quickly blend in two of the eggs, one after the other, continuing to stir until a really smooth paste is achieved.

Transfer the pastry to a piping bag with a 1 cm/^{1}/$_2$ in plain nozzle and pipe circles starting from the inside out like a snail's shell, no more than 5 cm/2 in in diameter on to a lightly oiled baking sheet, spacing them out so they do not stick to each other as they swell during cooking. This mixture will make 12 - 16 buns in total. Bake for about 15 minutes or until the buns are lightly golden. Leave to cool with the oven switched off and the door open.

To make the coffee icing, mix the coffee in a bowl with eight tablespoons of water and slowly add the icing sugar, beating until you have achieved a thick sauce consistency. If you find it is too thick add a little more water. Transfer to a pan and keep warm over a low heat.

To make the chocolate sauce, place two tablespoons of the cream in a pan with a tablespoon of water and bring to the boil. Remove from the heat and whisk in the grated chocolate to make a smooth sauce. Keep warm.

Whip the remaining cream and the vanilla in a bowl until soft peaks form and then use to fill the split buns. Arrange on one large serving platter or on individual plates. I like to swirl the chocolate sauce and the coffee icing over the top of each bun for a more dramatic effect.

I scamper along the beach, blissfully unaware that Greenpeace are watching my every move.

FEBRUARY

There was a time when we first opened the restaurant that the holiday in January was the only holiday of the year. Don't whinge I hear you say, plenty of people don't even get one. I know I'm as spoilt as Paris Hilton but descending the steps of the plane knowing there was a full 50 weeks of sweaty toil until the next adventure kept me feeling more than slightly sorry for myself. But now, happy days, we take a week in the autumn as well, so the holiday blues aren't quite as bad as they used to be. However, the small matter of reopening the restaurant always plays on my mind a few days before our return. I start wondering about supplies. I have my menu written before I go away. Each dish will also have been tried and tested, thereby minimising the confusion amongst the chefs. As usual my charts tell me what will, or should I say might, be available on our return, weather permitting.

The work load is always daunting on the first couple of days after we get back but we get into the swing of things soon enough. The kitchen is a cosy refuge from the weather outside. The grey skies and seemingly incessant rain can be hard to take after a couple of weeks in the Costa del whatever.

For a professional cook the buzz of the kitchen is part of the attraction. 'Sure anyone can cook' they say (excluding all the bravado of someone who has read *Kitchen Confidential* more than once) but what about cooking for 100 covers over a three hour session? This is the domain of the twenty-something chef, hungry for knowledge and relishing the school of hard knocks. There's a bit of that left in me but I don't have the stamina to keep up with the budding Ramsey's any more. I've done my time. After a hard night now I just want to go home and put on my slippers, not beer it up until the morning.

February seems to pass so quickly. Valentine's Day, of course, is the big one for the month. Nervous boys take out their girls, patently uncomfortable in a 'posh' restaurant, wanting to get on more familiar territory like the pub, the club or anywhere. I speak from experience so please don't think I'm patronising anyone – these kids pay my wages. So we look after these budding gourmands who might be our future regulars – from a little acorn grows a strong oak.

WHAT'S IN SEASON IN FEBRUARY

FRUIT apples, pears and rhubarb (forced) VEGETABLES artichokes (Jerusalem), beetroot, Brussels sprouts, cabbages, carrots, celeriac, chard, chicory, curly kale, leeks, mushrooms, onions, parsnips, potatoes, salsify, shallots, spring greens and turnips. FISH cod, black sole, grey mullet, haddock, halibut, lemon sole, oysters, scallops and turbot POULTRY duck, goose, guinea fowl and turkey GAME hare, pheasant, pigeon, rabbit, snipe and venison.

GUBBEEN PLATTER WITH MUSTARD AND PICKLED VEGETABLES

Not long ago I got a pressie of a little selection box of cured meat and salamis from Fingal Ferguson down in west Cork. His mother Giana makes the eponymous Gubbeen cheese. It is a classic case of 'if you buy well', or in this case cadge well – you need to do very little more to a good product. A little blob of Dijon mustard and some fine pickled vegetables were all it took to make this a hit. You can use any vegetables you like without going too mad - avoid green.

Serves 4 as a starter or light lunch

about 175 g / 6 oz selection of salamis, thinly sliced
175 g / 6 oz Gubbeen cheese, at room temperature
and cut into slices
about 4 tablespoons Dijon mustard or apple chutney
(see page 179 or good quality)

For the Pickled Vegetables

$1^1/_2$ teaspoons coriander seeds
200 ml / 7 fl oz white wine vinegar
100 g / 4 oz caster sugar
1 piece pared lemon rind
8 young carrots, scrubbed
2 small red onions cut into 5 mm / $^1/_4$ in rings
12 baby gherkins
crusty bread, to serve

To make the pickled vegetables, toast the coriander seeds in a small frying pan for a minute or two until aromatic. Place the white wine vinegar in a pan with the sugar, pared lemon rind and toasted coriander seeds. Bring to the boil, then reduce the heat and add the carrots, onions and gherkins. Cook over a gentle heat for 5 minutes, then remove from the heat and leave to cool completely. These can then be used straightaway or will keep for up to two weeks in a sterilised jar. Drain well from the liquid when ready to use.

Arrange the salamis and slices of Gubbeen cheese on a large platter. Add the drained pickled vegetables in small attractive mounds. A little dish of Dijon mustard or apple chutney and some good bread will complete the dish.

CROSTINI OF SMOKED DUCK WITH BUTTER BEAN, SAGE AND APPLE MUSTARD CREAM

Smoked duck on toast, that's essentially what this is. I don't see brushettas or crostini nearly as much as I used to. I think it was a 90's thing. Shame – fashion is such a fickle thing. Don't be tempted to make this too far in advance as the crostini will go soggy.

Serves 4 as a starter or light lunch

1 ciabatta loaf
1 garlic clove
2 tablespoons olive oil
75 ml / 3 fl oz cream
75 ml / 3 fl oz apple juice
pinch English mustard powder
8 fresh sage leaves, shredded
400 g / 14 oz can butter beans, drained and rinsed
1/2 lemon, pips removed
1 smoked duck breast, thinly sliced
salt and freshly ground black pepper

Preheat the grill. Cut the ciabatta loaf in half and then cut into 4 x 6cm / 2^1/$_2$ in x 4cm / 1^1/$_2$ in pieces – you'll only need two-thirds of the loaf so use the remainder in another dish. Cut the garlic in half and rub the pieces of ciabatta thoroughly with the cut side, then brush each one with the olive oil. Arrange on the grill rack and toast on both sides.

Meanwhile, place the cream in a pan with the apple juice and mustard, stirring to combine. Bring to the boil, then reduce the heat and simmer for a few minutes to thicken slightly. Add the sage and butter beans, stir well and allow to heat through. Season to taste and then add a squeeze of lemon. Keep warm.

Arrange the crostini on warmed serving plates and spoon over the butter bean mixture. Divide the smoked duck slices on top and serve at once.

JERUSALEM ARTICHOKES WITH LEEK, WALNUT AND PARMA HAM SALAD

Jerusalem artichokes make you fart. Well not me, you understand; either that or I fart so much anyway one or two more are nothing to be getting distressed about. Anyway I'm a big fan. This dish came about by accident and I'm glad it did.

Serves 4 as a starter or light lunch

6 tablespoons olive oil

8-10 Jerusalem artichokes, peeled and halved

2 garlic cloves, crushed

pinch chopped fresh sage leaves

16 walnut halves (fresh as possible)

2 small leeks, trimmed and cut into 1 cm / 1/2 in slices on the diagonal

1 tablespoon maple syrup

2 tablespoons red wine vinegar

juice of 1/2 lemon

8 slices Parma ham

salt and freshly ground black pepper

Preheat the oven to 180°C/350°F/Gas 4. Heat a small roasting tin and add two tablespoons of the olive oil. Add the artichokes, tossing to coat and cook in the oven for 10-15 minutes until golden brown and softish.

Add the garlic and sage to the tin and swirl it around, then tip the artichokes and garlicky oil into a bowl and set aside.

Place the walnuts on a baking sheet and toast for 4-5 minutes, then remove from the oven and leave to cool completely.

Blanch the leeks in a pan of boiling salted water for 2 minutes until just tender. Quickly refresh under cold running water, then gently squeeze out any excess liquid. Add to the artichoke mixture along with the maple syrup, red wine vinegar, lemon juice and the remaining olive oil, stirring gently to combine. Season to taste.

Divide the salad on to plates and scatter over the toasted walnuts, then drape the Parma ham around the edges of the plate. Leave at room temperature for 1 hour before serving.

ONE-POT CHICKEN WITH LENTILS AND RAISIN BROTH

This is my favourite type of cooking – deeply satisfying, easy and with very little washing up. Saturday afternoons seem to be the only time we eat at home these days. We have the morning off, we get the papers – head straight to the food supplement – then cook and eat in silence, thinking about the night ahead. If we're lucky we get a snooze, shower and head into work. The wonderful thing is that this dish couldn't be easier. Really it should be cooked in the oven after being brought up to a simmer but I appreciate not all ovens will take this large a pan so I've given both options.

Serves 4 – 6

1 kg / 2$^{1}/_{4}$ lb chicken, cleaned and trussed
(preferably free-range or organic)
4 small onions, cut in half
2 parsnips, cut into 3 cm / 1$^{1}/_{4}$ in slices
1 leek, trimmed and cut into 3 cm / 1$^{1}/_{4}$ in slices
2 carrots, cut into 3 cm / 1$^{1}/_{4}$ in slices
4 potatoes, cut into 3 cm / 1$^{1}/_{4}$ in cubes
4 garlic cloves, peeled
3 tablespoons puy lentils
2 tablespoons raisins
pared rind of $^{1}/_{2}$ lemon
sprig fresh thyme
pinch celery salt
1 teaspoon freshly grated horseradish or 1 tablespoon creamed horseradish
300 ml / $^{1}/_{2}$ pint cider
2 litres / 3$^{1}/_{2}$ pints chicken stock, plus a little extra if necessary (cubes are fine if you're stuck)
salt and freshly ground black pepper
olive oil, to garnish

Preheat the oven to 180°C/350°F/Gas 4 if you are going to finish the cooking of this in the oven. Place the chicken in a large pan with a tight-fitting lid and pack the onions, parsnips, leek, carrots, potatoes and garlic around it. Sprinkle in the lentils, raisins, lemon rind, thyme, celery salt and horseradish. Pour over the cider and chicken stock – the chicken won't be covered but don't worry as with the secure lid the steam will help the cooking process.

Bring the pan to a gentle simmer and either place in the oven for 1 hour or turn down the heat as far as it will go and cook for 45 minutes to 1 hour until the chicken and vegetables are completely tender. Remove from the heat and leave the chicken rest for a while. There's no harm in making this much earlier in the day and reheating it when the time comes to serve.

To serve, re-heat gently if necessary, then carve the chicken in the pan as best you can – this might be a little sloppy but don't worry, the taste is everything. Spoon the vegetables and broth into warmed serving bowls and arrange the slices of chicken on top. Season to taste and add a glug of olive oil to each one before serving.

POACHED SMOKED HADDOCK WITH CREAMY EGG SAUCE

I love egg mayonnaise. I love smoked haddock. I love rice. I love raisins. I love spring onions. OK, there's not much I don't like, but all these things point towards kedgeree. To make it look snazzy though I took it all apart for a perfect dish on our early bird menu – you can use shop-bought mayonnaise as long as it's not cheap rubbish but if you can make your own all the better. If you don't have or don't fancy saffron-flavoured rice just omit it; the rice will still be good. The sauce is meant to be served at room temperature.

Serves 4

450 ml / 3/4 pint milk

pinch black peppercorns

1 lemon wedge

1 sprig fresh thyme

3 sprigs fresh parsely

4 spring onions, trimmed

4 x 150 g / 5 oz natural smoked haddock fillets, boned

For the Sauce

small handful raisins

2 eggs

2 heaped tablespoons mayonnaise

1 tablespoon cream

1 teaspoon mango chutney

a little touch mild curry paste

1 shallot, finely chopped (or 2 tablespoons finely chopped onion if you don't mind a stronger taste)

For the Pilaff

350 g / 12 oz basmati rice

25 g / 1 oz butter

1 onion, finely chopped

pinch saffron strands

600 ml / 1 pint light chicken stock

1 bay leaf

salt and freshly ground black pepper

To make the sauce, place the raisins in a bowl and pour over enough boiling water to cover. Set aside to soak for at least 20 minutes, then drain and pat dry with kitchen paper. Place the eggs in a small pan and just cover with boiling water, then cook for 8-10 minutes until hard boiled. Drain, refresh under cold running water and remove the shells, then finely chop. Tip into a bowl and add the soaked raisins, mayonnaise, cream, mango chutney, curry paste, shallot or onion and mix until well combined. Season to taste, cover with cling film and chill until needed, remembering to allow it to come back to room temperature before using.

Preheat the oven to 180°C / 350°F / Gas 4. To make the pilaff, wash the rice thoroughly in a sieve and drain well. Melt the butter in an ovenproof pan with a tight-fitting lid and fry the onion until golden and translucent. Add the saffron and washed rice and stir gently over a low heat until well coated with the butter. Pour in the stock and bring to the boil, stirring occasionally. Add the bay leaf and season to taste, then put on the lid and place in the oven for 20 minutes. Remove from the oven and set aside for 5 minutes before removing the lid. The rice should be perfectly cooked and all the liquid should be absorbed.

Meanwhile, place the milk in a pan with the peppercorns, lemon wedge, thyme, parsley and spring onions and bring to a gentle boil. Slip in the smoked haddock and cover with a circle of non-stick baking parchment. Cook gently for 4-5 minutes or until the haddock is completely tender but still moist.

Tip the saffron rice out into a large warmed serving bowl and fork it through to make it fluffy. Spoon a couple of tablespoons of the sauce on to each serving plate and spread it out a little. Carefully remove the haddock and spring onions from the poaching milk and drain well on kitchen paper. Arrange the haddock on top of the sauce and garnish each one with a poached spring onion. Serve with the bowl of rice.

CRISPY LEMON SOLE & SOFT TARTARE MASH WITH WATERCRESS & LEMON

Lemon sole is a fantastic fish for deep frying, skin on or skin off. I sometimes skin it (get my fishmonger to do it really). I also treat it like black sole and grill it on the bone with whatever sauce or dressing takes my fancy. In this instance I'm coating it in the most perfect foolproof batter; even a monkey could make it. Indeed I've seen a few monkeys make it with great success. I love mashed potatoes and quite often transform them into a sauce-like consistency, killing two birds with one stone. Here I'm lashing the ingredients for the tartare sauce into the mash which replaces the mayonnaise.

Serves 4

grapeseed or sunflower oil, for deep frying
200 g / 7 oz self-raising flour
300 ml / 1/2 pint lager
8 large lemon sole fillets, skinned
bunch watercress, well picked over
a little olive oil
1/2 lemon, pips removed

For the Soft Tartare Mash

6 large floury potatoes, cut into chunks, such as Golden Wonders or King Edwards
85 ml / 3 fl oz milk (plus a little extra if necessary)
100ml / 31/2 fl oz cream
good knob butter
pinch capers, rinsed and finely chopped
6 gherkins, finely chopped
2 shallots, finely chopped
1 teaspoon Dijon mustard
salt and freshly ground black pepper
lemon wedges, to garnish

To make the soft tartare mash, cook the potatoes in a covered pan of boiling salted water for 15-20 minutes or until completely tender. Drain and pass through a mouli or potato ricer if you've got one; alternatively mash them as well as you can. Heat the milk, cream and butter in a small pan and then add to the potatoes a little at a time until well combined. We need to make the mash a little runny. If you need more liquid then just add more milk. Season to taste and fold in the capers, gherkins, shallots and mustard. Keep warm.

Meanwhile, heat the oil to 180°C/350°F for deep frying and make the batter. Sift the self-raising flour into a bowl with a pinch of salt. Make a well in the centre and pour in the lager, then quickly whisk together to make a smooth batter. Dredge the sole fillets through the batter, letting the excess drip off and deep fry for 11/2 minutes on each side until golden brown. Drain well on kitchen paper and season with salt.

Divide the soft tartare mash on warmed serving plates, remembering that it is also the carbohydrate so don't be mean. Place the watercress in a bowl and dress with a little olive oil and lemon, and season to taste. Arrange the crispy lemon sole on top of the mash and place the watercress on the side. Garnish with lemon wedges to serve.

CREAMED ARDSALLAGH CHEESE WITH HERBS

Ardsallagh is a soft creamy goats' cheese from Cork. I'm using it to make a soft cheese dip, bursting with herby flavours, to have with some crusty bread or garlic toasts at the end of a meal, or as a snack or a dip when friends come around.

Serves 4

250 g / 9 oz Ardsallagh goats' cheese
2 shallots, finely chopped
3 tablespoons chopped fresh mixed herbs
(chervil, flat-leaf parsley and chives)
glug olive oil
glug white wine
splash white wine vinegar
50 ml / 2 fl oz cream

For the Garlic Toasts

1 small French stick
1 garlic clove, peeled
olive oil, for brushing

To make the garlic toasts, preheat the grill. Cut the French stick into 1 cm/ $1/2$ in slices on the diagonal. Cut the garlic in half and rub the pieces of bread thoroughly with the cut side, then brush each one lightly with the olive oil. Arrange on the grill rack and toast on both sides. Don't be tempted to do these too far in advance or they'll go soggy.

Place the goats' cheese in a bowl and beat with a spatula for 2-3 minutes to lighten it. Beat in the shallots, herbs, olive oil, white wine, vinegar and season to taste.

In a separate bowl, whip the cream until soft peaks have formed and then gently fold into the cheese mixture. Transfer to a serving bowl, cover with cling film and chill until needed.

To serve, place the bowl of creamed Ardsallagh cheese with herbs on a large platter with the garlic toasts.

I recently went on a tumbling holiday in the French Alps (sorry, I meant skiing). Having torn some ligaments going at all of two miles an hour, I was incapacitated for four out of the seven days. These I spent eating cheese.

PEAR PECAN & PINE NUT TORTE WITH WHIPPED CREAM & MAPLE SYRUP

This is an adaptation of a recipe from Australian chef Philip Johnson's book. We discovered his restaurant, Ecco, in Brisbane by accident. We have this reputation amongst our friends for our holiday disasters. Whenever Mother Nature can interfere with our holiday it will: earthquakes in LA, hurricanes in Key West, plagues in India and cyclones in the Australian Northern tropics – yep, we've been there. After travelling thousands of miles around New Zealand and Australia, with numerous dodgy flights along the way, we decided to finish our holiday in the reputedly stunning Port Douglas, to chill out and soak up a few rays before our long journey home. Great, fine, fantastic. My thong was ready and I was prepared for my plump little body to be reddened like a freshly-boiled lobster. It wasn't to be. After a scorchingly hot few months, a cyclone was forecast, the first for three years – just our bloody luck. We hired a dinky studio apartment for the first three days. The rain and wind were so bad we had to join the local video club. Can you believe it? Membership no. 11350, by the way, if anyone wants to pretend they are me. We hopped out of Port Douglas during a lull in the storm and headed for the calm of Brisbane further south, which was undergoing a heat wave at the time. I was a sweaty little pony for three days there I can tell you, feeling sorry for myself until food, as usual, came to the rescue. The newly-rejunivated Centro District, with its trendy bars and brilliant cafés plus St James' Market which has an eye-popping selection of everything you could possibly want to eat, presented in a totally modern way. Most of all, however, in another part of Brisbane, gloomy and almost desolately situated is Ecco Bistro, casual, friendly and unpretentious, with amazing, simple food. I bought Philip Johnson's two books and I've been trying the recipes ever since.

Serves 10

6 ripe pears, peeled, cored, quartered and thinly sliced
grated rind and juice of 1 lemon
3 large eggs
250 g / 9 oz caster sugar
4 teaspoon vanilla extract
100 g / 4 oz butter
100 ml / 3^1/$_2$ fl oz milk
150 g / 5 oz plain flour
2 teaspoons baking powder
100 g / 4 oz pine nuts
100 g / 4 oz pecan nuts
125 g / 4^1/$_2$ oz sultanas, chopped
300 ml / ^{1}/$_2$ pint cream
icing sugar, to taste
maple syrup, for drizzling

For the Topping

3 tablespoons caster sugar
1 teaspoon ground cinnamon
1 teaspoon ground nutmeg

Preheat the oven to 170°C/325°F/Gas 3. Line the sides and base of a 26 cm / 10^1/$_2$ in spring form tin with non-stick baking parchment paper. Place the pears in a bowl with the lemon rind and juice and toss until well coated. This will prevent them from browning. Set aside.

Place the eggs, sugar and three teaspoons of the vanilla extract in a large bowl and whisk until pale and creamy. Melt the butter in the microwave or in a small pan and add the milk, then continue to whisk until well combined. Sift the flour and baking powder into a separate bowl and fold into the egg mixture.

Spread the pine and pecan nuts on a baking sheet and toast in the oven for about 5 minutes. Leave to cool and then chop the pecan nuts a similar size to the pine nuts. Scatter one third of the pears, nuts and sultanas over the base of the lined tin, then pour over one-third of the batter. Repeat this process until all the ingredients have been used up.

To make the topping, place the caster sugar, cinnamon and nutmeg in a bowl and mix well. Sprinkle over the top of the cake and bake for 1 hour and 20 minutes until well risen and golden brown. To test that it is has completely cooked through pierce the middle with a fine skewer – it should come out clean. Leave to cool in the tin for 5 minutes and then transfer to a wire rack to cool completely.

Whip the cream in a bowl with enough icing sugar to taste and the remaining teaspoon of vanilla extract. Cover with cling film and chill until needed. To serve, cut the torte into slices and arrange on serving plates, then drizzle over the maple syrup. Add dollops of the whipped cream to the side.

Thar's gold in them thar hills.

MARCH

The daffodils open after what seems an interminable wait, hopefully heralding the arrival of the bright, fresh days of spring. We seem to get the best of both worlds in our house, perched on the hills overlooking Dungarvan Bay. The drive from the town to my house is punctuated with sunbursts of yellow but ascending the hill the chillier air discourages the blooming for a few more weeks so when they open I can feast my eyes on their colour when all the flowers below me are an ugly brown mass of wilted leaves.

My thoughts at this time turn to staffing. Ours is a seasonal business, the highs and lows of different months necessitating different staffing levels. Summer is the big one, of course, and the little platoon of waiting staff swells to a small army, with college girls on holiday swelling the ranks. The chefs, however, are a different matter. Numerous phone calls are made to contacts in the business who are all invariably in the same boat. I won't use agencies, for that nonsensical and invariably huge charge might buy me a holiday or a coat of paint in the restaurant later in the year. Besides, if anybody's keen to work in a particular restaurant they should just apply.

The applications have always been slow enough. The good ones are few and far between. The hours certainly won't suit everybody and at that young age chasing the opposite sex comes very high on the agenda. For this they head to the bright lights of Dublin. I usually have to resort to cajolement, white lies and bluster. When I have a suitable applicant on my hook I lay it on thick and creamy. Raving like an overexcited advertising poster from the Wild West – *'thar's gold in them thar hills'* sort of thing.

The golf courses, the fishing, the beautiful scenery – oh forget that. The only scenery they want to concern themselves with are the 'chickitas' which I confidently assure them are amongst the finest in the land, as their sallow skin glistens in the balmy sub-tropical sunshine that we are blessed with in the sunny south east. This usually hooks them, and all the delights of Dungarvan become a rather moot point when they have to work like demons to feed the hungry hoards through the summer and the next time they catch slight of a woman is around September.

P.S. I know there are a lot of piggy dishes in this chapter but that's the kind of guy I am. I love the stuff and I was feeling pretty porcine while writing it. I make no apologies.

WHAT'S IN SEASON IN MARCH

FRUIT cooking and dessert apples, pears and rhubarb VEGETABLES Jerusalem artichokes, beetroot, sprouting broccoli, cabbages, carrots, chicory, cucumber, fennel, leeks, mushrooms, onions, parsnips, potatoes, sea kale, shallots, spring greens, turnips and watercress FISH brown trout, crab, hake, halibut, lemon sole, lobster, mussels, prawns, oysters, red mullet, salmon, sea bass, sea trout and shrimp.

MEDITERRANEAN FISH SOUP

I won't kid you. This soup requires a little extra effort but it's worth it. If you have ever eaten a classic French bouillabaisse, with its deep mysterious flavours and wonderous assortment of fish, plus the garlicky rouille spread on to garlic toasts adding a creamy hit to the endeavour, you know it is simply addictive. This soup can also be served on its own with a dollop of garlicky mayonnaise (aïoli) and some crunchy bread, or thin it down just a little or use it to poach your fish, red mullet, monkfish, prawns, mussels and gurnard accompanied with some boiled potatoes, French beans and good tomatoes. Heaven. N.B. The great plus with this soup is that although it makes a lot it freezes brilliantly.

Serves 10–12 as a starter or light lunch

50 ml / 2 fl oz olive oil

25 g / 1 oz butter

1 bulb fennel, trimmed and finely chopped

1 large carrot, finely chopped

1 onion, finely chopped

1 leek (white part only), finely chopped

4 celery sticks, finely chopped

2 garlic cloves, crushed

pinch fennel seeds

pinch black peppercorns

2 star anise

2 bay leaves

1 fresh rosemary sprig

900 g / 2 lb mixed whole fish, at least half of which needs to be red mullet – the rest can be gurnard, conger, rascasse and hake, scaled, cleaned and cut into 3 cm / 1¼ in pieces (get your fishmonger to do this for you)

2 glasses white wine

1 tablespoon tomato purée

400 g / 14 oz can chopped tomatoes

pinch saffron strands

2 pieces pared orange rind

dash brandy

dash Pernod

pinch cayenne pepper

salt, to taste

garlic toasts (see page 33), rouille (see Tip), and grated Gruyere cheese, to serve

Heat the olive oil in a large pan with the butter. Add the fennel bulb, carrot, onion, leek and celery and cook for 15-20 minutes over a medium heat until darkly caramelised, scraping frequently to remove sediment from the bottom of the pan and taking care not to burn the vegetables. Add the garlic, fennel seeds, peppercorns, star anise and herbs, stirring to combine. Add the fish and continue to stir over a low heat, then pour in the wine and add the tomato purée, chopped tomatoes, saffron and orange rind.

Pour 2½ litres / 4½ pints of water into the pan and bring up to a simmer, whilst scraping the bottom of the pan to remove any sediment. Cook gently for 45 minutes, then allow to cool a little and liquidise in batches. Pass through a strong sieve set over a large bowl, taking care to squeeze every bit of the juice and pulp through. This will take a little time. Cover with cling film and chill until needed.

To serve, return the soup to a clean pan to just heat through, taking care not to boil. Add the brandy, Pernod, cayenne pepper and season with salt to taste. Ladle into bowls and serve with separate dishes of the garlic toasts, rouille and Gruyere cheese.

TIP

To make rouille, place a seeded and chopped red pepper in a food processor or liquidiser with two crushed garlic cloves, 50 g / 2 oz of fresh white breadcrumbs, an egg yolk and a pinch of salt. Whiz until smooth and then with the motor still running, slowly add 150 ml/ ¼ pint of extra virgin olive oil as if making mayonnaise. When all the oil has been added, push the sauce through a sieve into a bowl. This will sit happily in the fridge covered with cling film for a couple of days.

ORANGE, FENNEL AND CHORIZO RISOTTO

It's no secret that I'm crazy about chorizo. You'll undoubtedly see it crop up more than once in this book. Risottos are a cinch. It's just a matter of deciding what flavour you want and then doing a little shopping. There's usually very little in our house to eat but we always have Arborio rice on hand. I'm not a stock Nazi. Use cubes – who has the time to make stock these days?

Serves 4–6 as a starter or light lunch

1 tablespoon sunflower oil
75 g / 3 oz butter
1 onion, finely chopped
1 small fennel bulb, trimmed and diced into 5 mm / 1/4 in cubes
100 g / 4 oz chorizo sausage, diced into 5 mm / 1/4 in cubes
400 g / 14 oz Arborio rice (risotto)
120 ml / 4 fl oz white wine
1.5 litres / 2 1/2 pints chicken stock
juice and finely grated rind 1 orange
finely grated rind 1/2 lemon
6 tablespoons freshly grated Parmesan
salt and freshly ground black pepper

Heat the sunflower oil in a sauté pan with 25 g / 1 oz of the butter. Add the onion and sweat for 3-4 minutes until cooked through but not coloured, stirring occasionally. Add the fennel bulb and chorizo and continue for cook for another few minutes. Tip in the Arborio rice and cook for 2 minutes, stirring until well coated and opaque in colour. Pour in the wine and allow to bubble down, stirring continuously until it has been completely absorbed.

Meanwhile, heat the stock and orange juice in a separate pan until just barely simmering. Once the wine has been absorbed stir a ladleful of the flavoured stock into the rice mixture and allow each stock addition to be almost completely absorbed before adding the next ladleful, until the rice is *al dente* – tender with a slight bite. This should take 15-20 minutes. Season to taste.

Stir the orange and lemon rind into the risotto with the rest of the butter and the Parmesan. Divide among warmed wide-rimmed bowls and serve immediately.

The best cooks cook by instinct – a dash of this, a ladle of that, teasing out the flavours from a dish; watching it evolve while maintaining a degree of restraint – knowing when to stop.

PEPPERED CHICKEN LIVERS WITH LEEK SALAD AND PEDRO XIMENEZ DRESSING

This is a great time of year for leeks. Pick ones that are green, firm and not too large, then wash well and trim most of the green leaves off. Pedro Ximénez is a dark, deep raisiny sherry that is fantastic with gamey flavours but it comes into its own when served with a chocolate dessert. Try soaking a few raisins overnight in a few glugs of this and the next day serve over vanilla ice cream – yum.

Serves 4 as a starter or light lunch

300 g /10 oz chicken livers (organic if possible)
2 leeks, well trimmed (see recipe intro.)
2 tablespoons olive oil
2 tablespoons plain flour
1 teaspoon cracked black pepper
1 capful sherry vinegar
2 capfuls Pedro Ximenez sherry (dark, sweet)
a little chopped fresh marjoram (optional)
Maldon sea salt

Clean the chicken livers and carefully remove the veins, keeping them whole. Cut off any green patches and discard, then wash and pat them dry with kitchen paper. Arrange on a plate and cover with cling film, then keep in the fridge for at least 30 minutes before you want to cook them.

Bring a large pan of salted water to the boil and cook the leeks for 4-5 minutes or until just soft but completely tender – this will depend on their size. Drain well and allow to cool on a clean tea towel. Pat away any excess water and then cut into 2 cm / 3/4 in rounds. Place in a bowl and season to taste.

Heat a cast iron or non-stick frying pan and add the olive oil. Place the flour on a shallow plate and mix in the cracked black pepper. Use to coat the chicken livers, shaking off any excess. When the oil is smoking, carefully add the chicken livers to the pan and cook for a couple of minutes until crisp and golden brown. Turn over and cook for another few minutes until just tender but still pink inside. Transfer to a warmed plate and leave to rest for a few minutes.

Divide the leeks among serving bowls and nestle the chicken livers on top. Return the pan to the heat and add the vinegar, scraping the bottom of the pan with a wooden spoon to remove any sediment. Pour in the sherry and then add the marjoram, if there's any available, and allow to bubble down which cooks out the alcohol, before spooning the sticky dressing over the leeks and chicken livers. Sprinkle with Maldon sea salt before serving for flavour and crunch.

CAESAR DRESSED SPROUTING BROCCOLI, CURED HAM AND GARLIC CROUTONS

This dish might outrage purists who maintain that the bastardisation of the classic Caesar salad is a curse but I use this famous dressing for a lot more than just to coat leaves of cos lettuce. Purple sprouting broccoli is a wonder. I can't get enough of it, literally. Tim, my veg man, grows it every year but I'm afraid demand is stronger than supply so when that inevitable call comes, no more left, I'm always as disappointed as if I've been dropped by a girlfriend I was particularly keen on. It's not the prettiest of vegetables. It's ungainly and hard to make look good on the plate but I've developed a laissez-fare attitude with this wonderful vegetable. Use any cured ham you like – Serrano, Parma, Bayonne, etc. This treatment of broccoli would be wonderful with some grilled cod or hake or even a bit of boiled bacon.

Serves 4 as a starter or light lunch

2 handfuls purple sprouting broccoli
8 slices cured ham (see recipe intro.)

For the Garlic Croutons

2 thick slices bread (good quality)
knob butter
1 garlic clove, crushed
pinch chopped fresh flat-leaf parsley

For the Caesar Dressing

1 tablespoon Dijon mustard
1 tablespoon red wine vinegar
$^1/_2$ garlic clove, crushed
150 ml / $^1/_4$ pint sunflower oil
150 ml / $^1/_4$ pint olive oil
50 g / 2 oz can anchovy fillets, drained and chopped
100g / 4oz freshly grated Parmesan
salt and freshly ground black pepper
roasted cherry vine tomatoes, to serve

Preheat the oven to 180°C / 350°F / Gas 4. To make the garlic croutons, cut the crusts off the slices of bread and discard, then cut the bread into cubes.

Place the butter in a baking tin with the garlic and pop into the oven for a minute or two until melted.

Add the bread cubes to the melted butter mixture and sprinkle over the parsley and seasoning to taste. Toss until well coated and then bake for 5-10 minutes until crisp and golden brown, tossing occasionally to ensure they colour evenly. Leave to cool and use as required.

To make the dressing, place the mustard in a food processor or liquidiser with the vinegar, garlic and two tablespoons of warm water. Season with pepper and blitz for about 10 seconds until blended. With the motor running, drizzle the sunflower and olive oil in through the feeder tube until you have achieved a thick consistency. Add the anchovy fillets and Parmesan and blend again until smooth. Pour into a sterilised jar or bottle and keep in the fridge for up to 1 week – you'll have plenty leftover to use in other dishes.

Plunge the broccoli into a pan of boiling salted water. Cook for 2-3 minutes or until tender, then refresh in iced water or run it under the cold tap. Drain well and place in a bowl. Add a couple of heaped spoonfuls of Caesar dressing and season to taste, then turn gently to coat. Divide amongst serving plates and drape the cured ham on top. Sprinkle over the garlic croutons and serve with some roasted cherry vine tomatoes.

If any fruit depends on the sun to bring out its flavour, it's the tomato. Buy deep red ones and BE FUSSY. The FCA would turn their noses up at those reddy green ones for grenade-lobbing practice, so don't even think about eating them.

BAKED HAM WITH ESTER HILL CHEESE CREAM AND CHIVES

I wanted to tell you about a cheese I just came across and put to good use. Ester Hill, an Irish Emmental from County Offaly, is one of the finest cheeses I've tasted for a long time – nutty and sweet. Wonderful for cooking with or eating on its own. This is an adaptation of a recipe from my very first cooking job, well, that doesn't include the chipper I worked in. It's old fashioned and a little too heavy on the calories but utterly delicious, especially with this new-found wonder cheese of mine. To cut down on its gut-bursting properties, serve it with a sharp green salad and a baked potato.

Serves 4–6

1.6 kg / 3^1/$_2$ lb half shoulder ham
knob softened butter
350 m l / 12 fl oz cream
pinch English mustard powder or 1 teaspoon prepared English mustard
150 g / 5 oz Ester Hill Emmental cheese, grated
freshly ground black pepper
snipped fresh chives, to garnish

Soak the ham overnight in a large pan of water. Refresh the water and bring to the boil, then reduce the heat and simmer gently for 1^1/$_2$ - 2 hours until tender. Leave to cool completely and then place in the fridge, loosely covered with cling film to set. This makes it much easier to slice and stops it from falling to bits.

Preheat the oven to 180°C / 350°F / Gas 4. Cut the ham straight from the fridge into 1 cm / ^{1}/$_2$ in slices. Grease a large casserole with the butter and arrange the slices of ham over the base in a slightly overlapping layer. Place the cream in a bowl and whisk in the mustard, then ladle over the ham, making sure to cover it completely. Sprinkle the cheese on top and season with pepper. Pop it in the oven for 15-20 minutes until it is golden brown and bubbling. Sprinkle with the chives and serve straight to the table.

BAKED SEA BASS WITH CAPERS, LINGUINI, PARSLEY AND GARLIC

I have to say that sea bass is without a doubt the most beautiful, delicious and noble of fish. Endangered in Irish waters in season, it is legal to catch two fish on a line per day, each fish being no smaller than fifteen inches. We therefore don't see a lot of sea bass and it's very expensive as a result but it's the business. Incidentally, farmed sea bass is now available, flown all the way from Greece so you know it's not going to be cheap, even for farmed. Apparently it's quite good but I am too much of a stingy knickers to pay a king's ransom for a fish that spends more time on a plane than I do. Don't worry if you can't find it – use hake, cod or even black pollock.

Serves 4

500 g / 1¼ lb linguini pasta
4 tablespoons olive oil
4 fresh sprigs thyme
4 x 175 g / 6 oz sea bass fillets, scaled
100 g / 4 oz butter
2 garlic cloves, crushed
4 shallots, finely diced
100 g / 4 oz fresh cep mushrooms (or another wild mushroom) trimmed and sliced
handful chopped fresh flat-leaf parsley
2 tablespoons crème fraîche
½ lemon, pips removed
Maldon sea salt and freshly ground black pepper
pinch of capers

Preheat the oven to 180°C/350°F/Gas 4. Place a large pan of water on to boil for the pasta and add a dash of the olive oil and a pinch of salt. Grease a baking tin with a little more of the oil and sprinkle with some salt and pepper. Place the thyme sprigs on top and lay the sea bass fillets over them. Drizzle with the remaining oil, break a little of the butter into tiny knobs and dot on top of the fish; then finally season to taste.

Heat half the remaining butter with half the garlic in a frying pan and sauté the shallots until softened and lightly golden. Tip into a bowl, then wipe the pan clean. Add the rest of the butter and garlic, then sauté the ceps for about 1 minute on each side over a high heat. Tip in the cooked shallots and the parsley, then toss to combine. Season to taste and remove from the heat.

Plunge the pasta into the pan of boiling salted water and cook for 8-10 minutes or according to packet instructions until *al dente* – just tender to the bite. Drain and reserve a little of the cooking water. Return the pasta to the pan and tip in the cep and shallot mixture. Toss well to combine and then stir in the crème fraîche and a little of the reserved cooking water if necessary. Keep warm.

Meanwhile, place the sea bass in the oven for 4-6 minutes until just cooked through and tender, depending on the thickness of the fish. Divide the pasta among warmed serving plates. Squeeze the lemon over the fish and arrange on top of the pasta, drizzling over any remaining juices from the baking tin and scatter the capers on top to serve.

45

*For some inexplicable reason I am extremely popular
with, ahem, shall we say the more mature ladies.*

JAMMY WHITE CHOCOLATE ROLL

This is really very easy and a good way to use a good quality jam or compôte to make a really delicious dessert. You might not fancy going to the bother of the jammy rhubarb compôte. I love it but use your favourite jam instead. It will still be gorgeous.

Serves 8

175 g / 6 oz white chocolate, grated
5 eggs
175 g / 6 oz caster sugar
icing sugar, to dust
300 ml / ½ pint cream
200 g / 7 oz jammy rhubarb compôte (see below) or shop-bought (see recipe intro.)

Preheat the oven to 180°C / 350°F / Gas 4. Line a 33 cm / 13 in x 23 cm / 9 in Swiss roll tin with non-stick baking parchment paper. Melt the white chocolate with three tablespoons of water in a heatproof bowl set over a pan of simmering water. Leave to cool a little.

Separate the eggs and place the yolks and whites in separate bowls. Add the caster sugar to the yolks and whisk until pale and thickened. Stir in the cooled chocolate mixture. With a clean whisk, beat the egg whites until stiff peaks have formed and then gently fold them into the chocolate mixture with a metal spoon. Pour into the prepared tin and bake for 15 minutes until well risen and slightly springy to the touch.

Remove the chocolate sponge from the oven and cover with a sheet of non-stick baking parchment paper. Leave to cool completely, even better overnight in the fridge.

When ready to serve, turn out the roulade on a fresh sheet of non-stick baking parchment paper dusted with icing sugar. Peel away the paper from the chocolate sponge. Whip the cream in a bowl until soft peaks have formed. Spread the compôte almost but not quite to the edges and then spread the whipped cream on top. Roll up carefully and dust with a little more icing sugar, before cutting into slices to serve.

TIP

To make your own jammy rhubarb compôte preheat the oven to 180°C / 350°F / Gas 4. You will need 450 g / 1 lb of strawberry jam to 700 g / 1 lb 9 oz of chopped rhubarb. Spread a layer of jam in the bottom of a pie dish or casserole. Cover thickly with rhubarb and add a little more jam. Fill to the top with the rest of the rhubarb. Finish with the remainder of the jam. Cover with tin foil and bake for 30-35 minutes. Allow to cool and transfer to sterilised jars. Use as required.

DAFFODIL SLICE AKA LEMON SUNBURST

Excuse me for the title. I know it's ultra cheesy but I'm getting into my Domestic Science mode. We ate these little babies on our trip to Australia a while back and Máire, who's the baker in the house, managed to nab the recipe. The baking in Oz was among the best I've ever tasted, all at once being classy, innovative and simple. These citrus delights are a gorgeous yellow line of soft translucent ultra white topping – that's where the reference to the daffodils comes from. I like these with a cup of tea in the afternoon ... Oh hell! I wish I was the paragon of restraint this suggests but I've had these for covert midnight feasts and furtive breakfasts too.

Makes about 8–10

150 g / 5 oz self-raising flour

175 g / 6 oz plain flour

325 g / 11^1/$_2$ oz icing sugar

250 g / 9 oz butter, cut into cubes

4 eggs

325 g / 11^1/$_2$ oz caster sugar

1 tablespoon finely grated lemon rind

120 ml / 4 fl oz freshly squeezed lemon juice

Preheat the oven to 170°C / 325°F / Gas 3. Line a 30 cm / 12 in x 20 cm/8 in baking tin with non-stick parchment paper, leaving a 2 cm / ^{3}/$_4$ in lip at the top of the tin.

Place the self-raising flour in a food processor with 150 g / 5 oz of the plain flour, a quarter of the icing sugar and the butter. Whiz until well combined and then spread into the bottom of the prepared tin. Bake for 20 minutes or until firm and set but not coloured.

Place the remaining 25 g / 1 oz of plain flour in a bowl with the eggs, caster sugar, lemon rind and half the lemon juice. Whisk until well combined and then pour over the set biscuit base. Return to the oven and bake for another 25-30 minutes until risen well and golden brown. Leave to cool completely.

Whisk the rest of the icing sugar and juice in a small bowl until smooth. Remove the tray bake from the tin and carefully remove the baking parchment. Spread the lemon icing over the top, allowing it to drizzle down the sides and leave to set, then cut into slices to serve.

I was indulged as a child. I used to suck on a lump of butter while watching telly. If anyone would take it off me, I would howl like a banshee until I got my greasy way.

APRIL

Each month has its own character. For me, Lent dominates April. Trying to understand the swings and shifts of these 40 days is beyond me. Nevertheless, it still has an impact in this Godless day and age.

I'm not a Bible basher, as you may have guessed, but there are a lot of people who cut down, if not cut out, during this period. Fish on Friday is not a strict rule but there is definitely an upsurge in interest during Lent. Of course, I try to give up some bad habits myself as well. I lasted nine days without beer last year. Nothing to boast about, I know, but for me it was a record. Long hot nights in the kitchen are not the same without a pint or two to break up the week. 'Yer man's got a problem', I can hear some of you howl in protest, and maybe you are right ,but try running around in a boiling kitchen for hours, or bent over with your head in a hot oven, being splashed by bubbling fat. The nerves jangle, the temper frays, and a cool pint seems a fair reward for such efforts, don't you think?

I tried giving up chocolate one year, and that was a joke. I only had to hear the rustle of a packet of chocolate biscuits being opened and I was there there like a bloodhound, drooling all over the place. Yes, I've got just about every vice known to man, well almost. I don't smoke and I don't do drugs, besides the occasional spliff when I was younger. They always made me queasy though. When I was told that my sickness would stop when I stopped drinking beer with it I gave the ganja the quick heave ho – so now I eat fast food, slow food, moderately quick food – just as long as I get food. I will never hold myself as a paragon of virtue. So roll on Easter Sunday, whatever day it falls on. We close due to the licensing laws on Good Friday. I don't mind. A day with friends is always a pleasure, contemplating how many Easter eggs I might get.

WHAT'S IN SEASON IN APRIL

FRUIT apples, seedless pink Muscat grapes, papaya and rhubarb VEGETABLES aubergine, broccoli, spring cabbage, carrots, cucumber, leeks, mushrooms, onions, potatoes, radishes, sorrel, spinach, rocket, turnip and watercress FISH brown trout, crab, halibut, lemon sole, lobster, monkfish, mussels, prawns, oysters, sea trout, shrimp and squid MEAT lamb.

CREAM OF ONION SOUP WITH APPLE JUICE AND THYME

You must try this soup. In the restaurant it's our fall back soup. If we have nothing else we always have onions. It's an all-year-round soup, with a texture of a creamy broth. The long, slow cooking of the onions is essential. This brings out the sweetness and concentrates the flavour. The trick is not to colour the onions at all so you need the lowest heat and a lid on top of the lot to trap the steam and keep the moisture inside.

Serves 4–6 as a starter or light lunch

good knob butter

2 large onions, thinly sliced

1 bay leaf

1.5 litres / 2^1/$_2$ pints chicken stock (from a cube will do)

100 ml / 3^1/$_2$ fl oz cream

glass apple juice (good quality)

pinch English powder or 1 teaspoon prepared English mustard

pinch chopped fresh thyme

salt and freshly ground black pepper

garlic croutons (see page 42) and grated Cheddar, to serve

Melt the butter in a large heavy-based pan with a tight-fitting lid and once it is foaming, add the onions and bay leaf, stirring to coat. Reduce the heat right down, cover with the lid and cook for 30-40 minutes until the onions are golden brown and caramelised, stirring once or twice.

Pour the stock into the onion mixture and bring to the boil, then reduce the heat and cook gently for another 10 minutes. Add the cream, apple juice, mustard, thyme and season to taste. Allow to just warm through and for all of the flavours to infuse. Ladle into warmed serving bowls and scatter over some garlic croutons and Cheddar to serve.

I rarely venture into the dining room, preferring the safe confines of the kitchen. In fact I am so averse to it, you have a greater chance of finding me pole dancing in Poland!

WARM SPAGHETTINI OF SQUID WITH CRUNCHY VEGETABLES

This is a great way to cook calamari. Slowly simmered in oil with the vegetables put in a few minutes before the end gives a lovely tender result. The crunchy vegetables temper the soft pasta and the colours are amazing – admittedly there is a little work in the vegetables but this mixture will keep for five to six days in the fridge. I then use it not only with pasta but over salads or on top of various risottos we might make.

Serves 4 as a starter or light lunch

100 ml / 3¹/₂ fl oz sunflower oil
100 ml / 3¹/₂ fl oz olive oil
4 garlic cloves, crushed
200 g / 7 oz fresh calamari or squid, cut into very thin slices – tentacles and all (frozen tubes will do)
1 carrot, cut into long thin strips (julienne)
1 small leek, trimmed and cut into long thin strips (julienne)
1 green and 1 red pepper, halved, seeded and cut into long thin strips (julienne)
handful chopped fresh flat-leaf parsley
handful chopped fresh dill
juice of 1 lemon
500 g / 1 lb 2 oz spaghettini or taglioni.
salt and freshly ground black pepper

Heat the sunflower and olive oil in a pan with the garlic to about 60°C/120°F – you should be able to put your pinky into it and keep it there for a few seconds. Add the squid and cook very slowly for 10–15 minutes until it is very soft. Add the carrot, leek, green and red peppers, then turn up the heat very slightly and cook for a further 5 minutes. Remove from the heat and stir in the herbs and lemon juice, then season to taste. Set aside until needed.

Bring a large pan of salted water to the boil and add a little of the oil from the squid. Plunge in the spaghettini or taglioni and cook for 6-8 minutes or according to the instructions on the packet until *al dente* – still slightly tender to the bite. Drain the pasta well and return to the pan. Tip in the squid and vegetable mixture and allow to just warm through. Divide among warmed serving bowls and serve immediately.

ROASTED WHOLE PRAWNS WITH SAFFRON MAYONNAISE

We were invited to a Grand National lunch at the house of some good customers of ours last year. I wasn't quite sure what sort of day it was going to be and was a little apprehensive. I've spoken about my ignorance around horses and the impact it has on my social life before (in my first book) so I won't blather on. Suffice to say it could have been a duck race as far as I was concerned. The house was magnificent - the drive seemingly almost as long as the road from my house to Dungarvan. We started with pink Champagne to fuel the anticipation – unfortunately, we were working that night so we were very much restricted in the wine department which was a shame because there was no super-market plonk being handed out here. Our mag-nanimous hosts ushered us into their kitchen to sit and eat one of the most memorable meals of the year, the starter of which I'm reproducing here. Langoustines like I've rarely seen the like of were heaped on to our plates so we rolled up our sleeves. This was proving to be a deliciously informal affair. We peeled, dipped and sucked from the seemingly never-ending supply of prawns – this lady knew her stuff, I thought. I ate my share and more – roast pork and butter beans followed for the main, then into the lounge for the Grand National where we entered a lottery, picked four horses each and threw a few euro into the pot. We all donned hats, bowlers, flat country caps and riding helmets, and started to roar at the telly. I sported a helmet with a whip to add a little extra flavour. Boy, those things sting. Needless to say all four of my horses fell but I didn't care. The prawns and the memory of a truly great day soothed me.

Serves 4 as a starter or light lunch

4 handfuls live Dublin Bay prawns (as large as you can buy – generosity is essential here)
a little olive oil

For the Saffron Mayonnaise

pinch saffron strands
2 egg yolks
$1/4$ teaspoon Dijon mustard
1 tablespoon white wine vinegar
175 ml / 6 fl oz sunflower oil
splash extra virgin olive oil
1 tablespoon crème fraîche (optional)
a little fresh lemon juice
salt and freshly ground black pepper
lemon wedges, to serve

To make the saffron mayonnaise, place the saffron in a small bowl and cover with a little boiling water. Set aside to soak. Place the egg yolks in a bowl with the mustard, a pinch of salt and the white wine vinegar.

Place the oils in a measuring jug and gradually dribble into the egg yolks, whisking continuously – it may help to sit the bowl on a damp cloth while doing this. After a minute or so you will notice the mixture beginning to thicken. When this happens add the oil a little faster but not too fast or the mixture will suddenly curdle.

Once all the oil is added to the egg yolk mixture, remove the whisk and fold in the saffron mixture and crème fraîche, if using a spatula. Season to taste and add the lemon juice to taste. Cover with cling film and chill for at least 1 hour before using as this will give the saffron time to secrete all of its colour and flavour. When you see this happening, give the mayonnaise a little stir to amalgamate.

Preheat the oven to 220˚C / 425˚F / Gas 7. Spread the prawns out as evenly as possible in a large roasting tin and drizzle with the olive oil. Season to taste and roast for 8-10 minutes until just tender. Heap the prawns on to warmed serving plates and spoon the saffron mayonnaise into small ramekins on the side. Add a wedge of lemon, roll up the sleeves and dig in.

ESCALIVADA WITH BUFFALO MOZZARELLA

You may have guessed that this is one of Joseph's recipes; 'typical Catalan' is what he used to say about virtually everything he cooked. I was happy to let him at it. We served this with a salt cod cream seen on page 11 but it's good with almost anything; lamb, beef, rabbit or any kind of fish but particularly seared fresh tuna. Indeed stick a little goats' cheese or feta on top and you have a fine salad. Put it on a chargrilled bit of ciabatta and it makes fine crostini. Alternatively put some in a wrap or sandwich with some buffalo mozzarella and basil. Hey presto!

Serves 4 as a starter or light lunch

1 large onion, peeled

4 tablespoons olive oil, plus extra for drizzling

4 garlic cloves, peeled

1 aubergine

2 red peppers

1 tablespoon white wine vinegar

1 tablespoon chopped fresh flat-leaf parsley

6 canned anchovies, drained and roughly chopped (optional)

2 buffalo mozzarella, sliced

12 black olives (good quality)

salt and freshly ground black pepper

Preheat the oven to 180°C/350°F/Gas 4. Place the onion on a piece of foil, drizzle over a little of the olive oil and season to taste. Wrap up securely and place on a baking sheet, then roast for 30 minutes until almost tender.

After 30 minutes open the onion parcel and add the garlic cloves, reseal and roast for another 15 minutes until completely tender. Place the aubergine and red peppers in a roasting tin and then drizzle over a little of the olive oil. Season to taste and then roast for about 20 minutes, turning occasionally. Remove the vegetables from the oven and allow to cool completely, reserving any juices.

Drain any juices from the roasted vegetables into a large bowl and add the rest of the olive oil. Place the white wine vinegar into a small bowl and microwave for 30 seconds. Alternatively you can heat it in a small pan – this softens the vinegar and brings out the flavour. Add to the olive oil mixture. Finely chop the roasted garlic and add, along with the parsley, stirring to combine.

To prepare the roasted vegetables, peel the roasted red peppers and remove the stalks and seeds, then cut the flesh into 2.5 cm / 1 in chunks. Peel the aubergine and cut into similar-sized chunks, along with the onion, as best you can. Fold into the olive oil mixture with the anchovies, if using. Season to taste, cover with cling film and chill until needed. It will keep well in the fridge for up to 1 week.

To serve, arrange the escalivada on serving plates and allow to come back up to room temperature if it has been chilled. Arrange the sliced mozzarella on top and scatter over the olives, then give a good drizzle of olive oil to each one.

SLOW ROAST LAMB, IRISH RATATOUILLE AND MINTED YOGHURT

I recently got Sky, and whilst slumped on the couch one evening I was watching one of Nigella Lawson's programmes. She cooked a shoulder of lamb overnight and the next day she shredded it and served it with a salad, mint and pomegranate. It was so utterly fabulous I almost started licking the telly. I'm adapting this for what I would like to eat for Easter Sunday lunch. I'm forever saying that it should never be only about the finest, as in the most expensive cuts. The racks and fillets of this world come a distinct second to dishes like this. The Irish ratatouille is a little tongue in cheek. Roasted root vegetables and potato mixed with aubergines, peppers and courgettes, then bound in a spiced tomato sauce, may sound a little odd but do try it. It's wonderful.

Serves 6–8

2.5 kg / 5¹/₂ lb shoulder of lamb, bone intact
a little olive oil
1 bulb garlic, skin on and cut in half
1 bunch fresh rosemary
8 tablespoons natural yoghurt
1 bunch fresh mint, chopped

For the Tomato Sauce

2 x 400 g / 14 oz cans chopped tomatoes
2 tablespoons olive oil
3 shallots, thinly sliced
4 garlic cloves, finely chopped
1 teaspoon cumin seeds
2 teaspoons chopped fresh rosemary or thyme
pinch caster sugar

For the Irish Ratatouille

handful raisins
2 carrots
1 parsnip
1 small turnip
4 potatoes
good splash olive oil
2 red peppers
1 aubergine
2 courgettes
salt and freshly ground black pepper

You'll need to start this early if you are going to serve it for lunch. It will take 5 hours in a preheated oven at 170°C / 325°F / Gas 3 or stick it in the oven overnight like Nigella at 140°C / 275°F / Gas 1 and just put it back in a hottish oven to reheat. Heat a large roasting tin with the olive oil directly on the hob and use to brown the lamb fat side down. Add 500 ml / 18 fl oz of boiling water with the garlic and rosemary. Season the lamb well and cover securely with foil. Place in the oven according to the instructions above and cook until meltingly tender.

To make the tomato sauce, blitz the cans of tomatoes in a food processor or liquidiser to a purée. Heat the oil in a heavy-based pan. Tip in the shallots, garlic and cumin and sauté for about 5 minutes until softened but not coloured. Add the puréed tomatoes and herbs, then reduce the heat and simmer for 45 minutes or until the tomatoes are well reduced, stirring occasionally so the sauce does not catch on the bottom of the pan. Season to taste and add the caster sugar. Set aside until ready to use – this can be made well in advance and kept covered with cling film in the fridge until needed.

Increase the oven temperature to 200°C / 400°F / Gas 6. Place the raisins in a bowl and pour over enough boiling water to cover. Set aside for at least 20 minutes but the longer the better. Drain and pat dry with

kitchen paper before using. Cut the carrots, parsnip, turnip and potatoes into 5 cm / 2 in x 1 cm / ¹/₂ in even-sized batons. The cutting of the vegetables is important as the regularity is needed to cook them evenly. Tip all the vegetables into a large roasting tin and drizzle over half the olive oil, turning to coat. Season to taste and roast for 15 minutes, stirring carefully once or twice to ensure even cooking.

Meanwhile, cut the red peppers, aubergine and courgettes in the same fashion, discarding the seeds and stalks. Add them to the root vegetables and drizzle over the remaining oil, tossing to coat. Return to the oven for another 10 minutes and then pour over the tomato sauce and tip in the soaked raisins. Season to taste and bake for another 10 minutes or until all

the vegetables are completely tender. This can be used immediately or allowed to cool, so the sauce has a further opportunity to penetrate the vegetables, and then reheated in a hottish oven with the lamb when ready to serve.

To make the minted yoghurt, place the yoghurt in a bowl and stir in the mint. Season to taste and cover with cling film. Chill until ready to use.

To serve, place a spoonful of the ratatouille in the centre of warmed, wide-rimmed serving bowls and spoon off a hunk of lamb – literally there is no carving here – it may look a little messy but tastes divine. Drizzle over some minted yoghurt and away you go.

MUSSEL FEAST

This is a version of the big pot of mussels I featured in the last book: quite positively the easiest way to cook mussels and get a delicious sauce to boot. Again, I'm using chorizo. I just love the stuff. You could use smoked bacon or no meat at all for that matter. This recipe is just a guide but you could use any combination you fancy providing you retain some sort of sanity and don't start popping in some passion fruit or another zany component in your quest to find a few fusion food. I love the idea of a French raclête, one central dish and a few others to complement and enhance it. All this ferreting around leads to an atmosphere of conviviality and breaks the ice. For this I would recommend lots of good bread to soak up the juices, boiled new potatoes with chives, marinated cherry tomatoes and a crisp green salad. Place the pot in the middle of the table and dig in.

Serves 4

2 kg / 4¹/₂ lb mussels, well cleaned
good glug white wine
1 onion, finely chopped
2 garlic cloves, crushed
200 g / 7 oz cooked chorizo, cut into 5 mm / ¹/₄ in dice
3 bay leaves
2 teaspoons smoked paprika (if not available use ordinary)
250 ml / 9 fl oz cream
1 orange
2 tablespoons chopped fresh flat-leaf parsley

For the Marinated Cherry Tomatoes

225 g / 8 oz cherry tomatoes, halved
1 large onion, halved and thinly sliced
50 ml / 2 fl oz balsamic vinegar
75 ml / 3 fl oz olive oil
50 g / 2 oz capers, well rinsed
2 garlic cloves, crushed
drizzle honey
salt and freshly ground black pepper
boiled new potatoes with chives, crisp green salad and some crusty bread, to serve

To marinate the cherry tomatoes, place the tomatoes in a large, non-metallic bowl and add the onion, balsamic vinegar, olive oil, capers, garlic and honey. Season to taste and stir well to combine, then place in a warm place for at least 1 hour so the tomatoes soften slightly and all the flavours are given a chance to infuse. These can also be kept covered with cling film in the fridge for 2-3 days.

Place the mussels in a very large pan with a tight fitting lid and add the wine, onion, garlic, chorizo, bay leaves, paprika and cream. Pare in the rind of half the orange and then squeeze in all the juice. Put on the lid and bring to the boil on the fastest gas or electric ring you have. After 3-4 minutes they should start to steam. Dig around with a wooden spoon as quickly as you can and put the lid back on. Cook for another 3-4 minutes, until all of the mussels have opened.

To serve, sprinkle the parsley over the mussels and put on the table with a ladle so everyone can fish around for a nice balance of mussels and juice. I like to eat the juice first leaving a little at the end to soak up with your bread. Serve with bowls of the boiled new potatoes with chives, marinated cherry tomatoes and a crisp green salad for a fantastic feast.

FRIED LEMON SOLE, EGGY PARMESAN CRUST AND RISOTTO OF PETIT POIS

I use lemon sole a lot. In this case it is dredged in a mixture of beaten egg, herbs and finely grated Parmesan, and cooked briefly in a hot pan until it forms an omelette-like coating around the fish that is cheesily delicious. I'm not getting all fancy pants on you by having a bit of French in the title, but there are frozen garden peas and the daintier more tender petit pois. Either is a great staple to have in the freezer. If you fancy put a little bacon in your risotto for an extra oomph.

Serves 4

4 eggs
splash milk
handful freshly grated Parmesan
pinch snipped fresh chives
pinch paprika
splash olive oil, plus a little extra for drizzling
good knob butter
8 large lemon sole fillets

For the Risotto

1 litre / 1³/4 pints fish or light chicken or ham stock (a stock cube will do)
pinch chopped fresh mint
knob butter
1 small onion, finely chopped
275 g / 10 oz Arborio rice (risotto)
100 g / 4 oz frozen petit pois (about 1 cup)
2 tablespoons crème fraîche
salt and freshly ground black pepper
lemon wedges, to garnish

To make the risotto, place the stock and mint in a pan and heat to just below simmering point. In a separate pan, melt the butter until foaming and add the onion, then cook for a couple of minutes until soft and translucent. Add the rice and stir for a minute or two until all is nicely coated in the butter. Start by adding the stock, ladle by ladle, each time making sure the previous ladle has been completely absorbed before adding the next, stirring continuously. The whole process should take 15-20 minutes. When the rice is almost ready, add the petit pois and season to taste, then stir in the crème fraîche.

Meanwhile, cook the lemon sole. You will have to cook this in batches and transfer to a warm plate in the oven. Break the eggs into a shallow dish and add the milk, Parmesan, chives, paprika and season to taste, then lightly whisk to combine. Heat the oil and butter in a non-stick frying pan until foaming. Dip some of the fillets in the egg mixture. Coat them thoroughly and shake off any excess egg before putting as many fillets as you comfortably can in the pan. Cook for 2-3 minutes on each side until the fish is golden brown, then transfer to the oven and repeat the process until all the fish is cooked.

Place a good spoonful of the risotto on each warmed serving plate and arrange the lemon sole fillets on top. Drizzle with a little extra olive oil and garnish with lemon wedges to serve.

BAKED CARAMEL CUSTARD WITH HOT APPLE FRITTERS AND MAPLE SYRUP

I love fritters of any kind. I use these ones to dip into the caramel pots almost like a fondue. If you fancy bananas work away or pears are good too. Just make sure your pears are ripe. The cold custard and hot fritters add an extra dimension to this delicious dish.

Serves 6

sunflower oil, for deep frying
225 g / 8 oz self-raising flour
300 ml / 1/2 pint lager
2 Granny Smith apples, peeled, cored and each cut into 6 pieces
2 tablespoons caster sugar
maple syrup, for drizzling

For the Caramel Custard

225 g / 8 oz caster sugar
250 ml / 9 fl oz milk
500 ml / 18 fl oz cream
7 egg yolks

Preheat the oven to 130°C / 250°F / Gas 1/2. To make the caramel custard, place the caster sugar in a heavy-based pan with 50 ml / 2 lf oz of water. Heat gently, stirring occasionally until the sugar dissolves, then bring to the boil and cook for about 5 minutes until you have achieved a golden caramel, without stirring.

Meanwhile, place the milk and cream in a separate pan and just warm through but do not boil. Add this to the caramel carefully as it will spit, then stir well to combine. Beat the egg yolks in a bowl until pale and gradually whisk into the hot caramel. Strain through a fine sieve into a jug and then use to fill 6 x 7.5 cm / 3 in ramekins that are x 5 cm / 2 in high. Place in a bain marie (roasting tin half filled with boiling water) and bake for about 50 minutes or until the custard is just set but still has a slight wobble in the middle. Leave to cool completely, then chill until needed. These are even better if made the day before.

Heat the oil to 170°C / 325°F in a deep fat fryer or deep-sided pan, just be careful if it's the latter. Sieve the flour into a bowl and make a well in the centre, then tip in the lager and beat together until you have achieved a smooth batter. Dip some of the apple slices into the batter, shaking off any excess and carefully drop into the heated oil. You may have to do this in two batches so they don't stick together. Cook for 2-3 minutes until golden brown. Place the caster sugar on a flat plate. Quickly drain the fritters on kitchen paper and toss in the caster sugar to lightly dust.

To serve, place each custard pot on a serving plate and arrange a pile of two fitters next to each one. Drizzle a little maple syrup on top of the fritters.

They looked as though they had just stepped off the pages of Kitchen Confidential: mean, dangerous and utterly shagged.

MAY

You can almost smell the summer. Tim, my ever-present veg man, rings and tells me what's flourishing in his garden and I plan my menus around that. The better weather and longer evenings always provoke me into lightening the food – no more need for comfort. Vitality and vibrant colours abound and the food reflects this. I start to swap the cream sauces for olive oils, pestos and dressings. People don't want to feel as if they have consumed a small child for dinner. Full but content is my mantra.

I've recently returned from a trip to Madrid. As usual I have my nose in a guidebook for a couple of weeks beforehand. Unusually I booked a couple of two-Michelin-starred restaurants. This kind of star chasing I leave to others but these aroused my curiosity. The first chef was a disciple of Ferran Adria who is without a doubt a genius, but unfortunately I have never eaten in his restaurant, El Bulli. I won't mention the name of this protégé's

restaurant because I'm about to slag the place. The clinically Spartan décor had about as much charm as a hospital ward and the food, while at times showing flashes of ingenuity that were technically beyond my capabilities, had worrying similarities to the worst days of Nouvelle cuisine. No wonder I'm at my happiest in noisy bistros where the food is honest, perhaps a little old fashioned, but solidly dependable. I left, a little miffed, to say the least.

The next night I was apprehensive. Was it going to be more of the same, big bucks for a big disappointment? We went to Santceloni anyway, thank God, for it was thrillingly exceptional; plush but modern with a veritable army of waiters who were friendly but courteous, and served stunningly accomplished food. It cost a bit but I didn't mind, because it was sheer theatre. The duck and chickens were carved at a central table after being presented to the salivating customer. A glistening silver duck press was shunted carefully to and from the kitchen to be cleaned and polished before the juice of the next roast duck was pressed from its gleaming spout. The apparatus sported a wheel mounted on its turret that resembled a machine from a Jules Verne novel. It took three bulky waiters to extract this nectar: one to turn the wheel, and the others to hold the weighty contraption.

There is something egalitarian about the Spanish food culture. It seems to be all things to all people. Workers rub shoulders with fur-coated dames. Leathery hands clutch glasses of Cervesa with stubby blackened fingers, the men silently wolfing down lamb chops while beside them, beautifully manicured hands elegantly swirl glasses of Cava while gossiping to bejewelled lady friends.

I witnessed a mahogany-like veal shank being ferried gracefully past me to receive acclamation from two lucky carnivores, and taken away, again to the central table. The bone was slipped out from the shank, the meat divided and then set on soft mashed potato, with just a little gravy. The lucky boys tucked in. I wasn't disappointed though with my crispy neck of pork and crushed broad beans. This was lip-smackingly, yum-suckingly gorgeous. Máire's sweetbreads were likewise – I could go into the whole meal but then you would realise what a glutton I am. I felt like the fat guy in Monty Python's movie, 'The Meaning of Life', when he ate one mint too many and burst. So much for my mantra. My point is that Santceloni on the Paseo de la Castellana, for those of you who want to go there, has entered my top-five restaurants. It is not because is has two stars in the Michelin Guide, since my number two is Bar Pinotxo in the Boqueria market in Barcelona.

The first restaurant was half empty – this in a major capital city on a Thursday night – whilst Santceloni was thronged. Cook what people want to eat is the message. The cerebral scientific stuff is for others. I cannot do what they do but nor do I want to. You are probably asking yourself, what's this got to do with May – nothing other than it was then that I visited Madrid.

WHAT'S IN SEASON IN MAY

FRUIT apples, cherries, gooseberries, and rhubarb VEGETABLES asparagus, beetroot, broad beans, broccoli, cauliflower, carrots, cucumber, kohlrabi, lettuce, new potatoes, rocket, samphire, and watercress FISH brown trout, crab, haddock, lemon sole, monkfish, plaice, sardines, sea bass, sea trout, shrimps POULTRY duck MEAT new season lamb.

ASPARAGUS WITH CREAMY GOATS' CHEESE, APPLE AND MINT DRESSING

I'm going to use asparagus a lot in the restaurant this month, as it's a short season and I want to make the most of it. For a start I'm going to serve it in a number of different ways whether that be roasted, steamed or boiled. My favourite way is served simply warmed with a soft, freshly-poached egg, lots of melted butter, Maldon sea salt and fresh pepper. Simple but effective. I was playing around with some goats' cheese one day and came up with this recipe for a tangy delicious dressing that the asparagus sits on. How many asparagus you eat depends on the size of them and how badly you crave them so I've just given a rough guide here – feel free to increase or decrease as the mood takes you.

Serves 4 as a starter or light lunch

20 asparagus spears
knob butter
100 g / 4 oz Ardsallagh goats' cheese (soft and mild)
85 ml / 3 fl oz apple juice (good quality)
6-8 fresh mint leaves
1 garlic clove, chopped
Maldon sea salt and freshly ground black pepper

It is important to trim and peel your asparagus carefully. I've seen a lot of waste in my time. Cut or snap the asparagus where it starts to get woody, then peel with a light hand about 4 cm / 1 1/2 in from the tip of the base. Place the asparagus in a steamer or into a large pan of boiling salted water for 2-4 minutes, depending on their size. Plunge into iced water and once they have cooled down, transfer to a clean tea towel and allow to drain completely. Arrange on a flat plate and cover with cling film, then chill for up to 4 hours until needed.

Place the goats' cheese in a mini blender or liquidiser with the apple juice, mint and garlic. Whiz until well combined and then season to taste. Transfer to a bowl and cover with cling film, then chill until needed.

To serve, heat a large frying pan and add the butter. Once foaming, tip in the asparagus and sauté for about 2 minutes until heated through. Spoon the goats' cheese dressing into the middle of each serving plate and arrange the asparagus on top.

TIP

Leeks and asparagus go hand in hand so if you want to mix nice young leeks cooked the same way with your asparagus it would be a great combination. It is also worth considering investing in a ridged frying (griddle) pan as an addition to your kitchen. Try brushing the asparagus with a little oil and chargrilling them.

ASIAN LAMB SALAD

These days I try and keep my cooking as close to home as possible, avoiding the Pacific Rim fusion eating that can be so badly done in the wrong hands, but there are certain flavours I can never turn my back on; ginger, sesame, soy with a hint of chilli always gets me going. Whether with fish or almost any kind of meat, it's a sure winner. I use this dressing often with crab and even salmon. See Oriental crab risotto in August (page 117). It's a great standby and lasts for a couple of weeks in the fridge. Rump of lamb is my favourite cut. It's a nugget of meat at the top end of the leg that a lot of Irish butchers use for chump chops. If you cannot find this use lamb loin.

Serves 4 as a starter or light lunch

a little sunflower oil, plus extra for drizzling
2 x 225 g / 8 oz rumps of lamb
4 little gem lettuces
4 spring onions, trimmed and shredded
1/2 cucumber, peeled, seeded and cut into thin batons
pinch toasted sesame seeds

For the Dressing

100 ml / 3 1/2 fl oz light soy sauce
2 tablespoons toasted sesame oil
few drops sweet chilli sauce
1 teaspoon honey
1 small garlic clove, crushed
splash rice wine or white wine vinegar
1 tablespoon finely chopped pickled ginger (optional)
Maldon sea salt and freshly ground black pepper

Preheat the oven to 180°C / 350°F / Gas 4. Heat a heavy-based frying pan with a splash of the sunflower oil until smoking. Season the lamb and put it in the pan skin side down. It might spit so be careful. Allow to crispen up for 2-3 minutes, then pop it in the oven for 10 minutes. Turn over and cook for another 2-3 minutes. Transfer to a plate and leave to rest for 10 minutes. I cook my lamb medium-rare and I would certainly not cook it more than medium.

Meanwhile, make the dressing. Place the soy sauce in a bowl with the sesame oil, chilli sauce, honey, garlic, rice wine or white wine vinegar and pickled ginger, if using. Whisk until well combined, then reserve.

Pull apart and wash the little gems, then scatter over a deep serving dish. Cut the rested lamb into thin slices and arrange on top. Mix the juices on the plate into the dressing and then spoon on top. Scatter over the spring onions, cucumber and sesame seeds. Season to taste and serve at once.

POTATO CAKES WITH SMOKED MACKEREL, MANGO AND CUCUMBER DRESSING

I really wanted to include this recipe. They are called *pomme dauphine* in classical terminology and they've been around a lot longer than I have – please don't be put off by the fact you have to make choux pastry for this is what gives them their incredibly light texture. Use these babies as a vehicle for any meat or fish you like. I sometimes serve them with roast beef or lamb, or sauté some wild mushrooms and nestle them on top; with poached or scrambled eggs and bacon, they make an unsurpassable brunch. If you like the dressing it's also great with pork or chicken.

Serves 4 as a starter or light lunch

100 ml / 3¹/₂ fl oz cream

2 tablespoons white wine vinegar

1 teaspoon prepared English mustard

¹/₄ teaspoon mild curry paste (optional)

1 ripe mango, peeled, stoned and diced

pinch chopped fresh mint

¹/₂ cucumber, peeled, seeded and diced

2 large smoked mackerel fillets, bones removed

For the Potato Cakes

110 g / 4¹/₄ oz butter

225 g / 8 oz plain flour, sifted

6 eggs, beaten

16 new potatoes

600 ml / 1 pint sunflower oil

Maldon sea salt and freshly ground black pepper

To make the potato cakes, place the butter in a pan with 275 ml / 9¹/₂ fl oz of water and a pinch of salt, then bring to the boil. As soon as it reaches boiling point, tip in the flour and stir with a spoon over the heat until the mixture comes away from the sides of the pan. Leave this to cool to blood temperature, then gradually mix in the beaten eggs until well combined.

Meanwhile, cook the potatoes in a pan of boiling salted water for 12-15 minutes or until tender, then drain and when cool enough to handle, peel.

Crush the peeled potatoes with a fork and then mix them with the choux pastry – you are looking for the consistency of two-thirds potato to one-third choux pastry. Press into a 8 cm / 3¹/₄ in round cutter set on a baking sheet lined with non-stick baking parchment paper (or use a smaller cutter if that's all you have). Repeat until you have four potato cakes in total. Cover with cling film and chill until needed. These will keep for up to one day in the fridge.

To make the dressing, place the cream in a bowl with the white wine vinegar, mustard and curry paste if you'd like a bit of a kick. Whisk until well combined, then stir in the mango, mint and cucumber.

When you are ready to serve, heat the oil in a deep sided pan to 180°C / 350°F. Deep fry the potato cakes for 3-4 minutes until crisp and golden brown. Drain well on kitchen paper and place one in the centre of each warmed serving plate. Cut each smoked mackerel fillet neatly in half and arrange on top, then spoon over some of the dressing. Spoon a little more around the edge of each plate to serve.

ROAST BELLY OF PORK, BEETROOT TSATZIKI AND ROCKET

I adore belly of pork and I pretty much serve it all year round in various guises, this being one example. I'm a big fan of beetroot and try to incorporate it into my menus as much as possible. This dish has a springtime feel. If you don't fancy the beetroot, try serving the pork with the roasted winter vegetables and spiced crème fraîche (see page 158).

Serves 4

1 large onion, sliced into rings
4 garlic cloves, finely chopped
1 bunch fresh sage, chopped
300 ml / ½ pint chicken stock
1.5 kg / 3 lb pork belly, rind removed
150 ml / ¼ pint dry cider
8 whole cloves
pinch ground allspice
pinch ground cinnamon
75 g / 3 oz Demerara sugar
2 handfuls rocket
1 tablespoon red wine vinegar
2 tablespoons olive oil

For the Beetroot Tsatziki

3 cooked beetroot, peeled and grated
1 Granny Smith apple, peeled, cored and grated
200 ml / 7 fl oz Greek yoghurt
2 garlic cloves, crushed
2 tablespoons red wine vinegar
2 tablespoons olive oil
1 freshly grated horseradish or 1 teaspoon creamed horseradish
Maldon sea salt and cracked black pepper
roast potatoes, to serve (optional)

Preheat the oven to 150°C / 300°F / Gas 2. Place the onion rings in a single layer in the bottom of a roasting tin. Sprinkle over the garlic and half of the sage, then pour in the stock. Sit the pork belly on top, then splash over the cider. Sprinkle over the remaining sage with the cloves, allspice and cinnamon. Season to taste and cover with foil. Bake for 3 hours until the pork is completely tender and very soft, basting occasionally. Remove the foil and sprinkle the Demerara sugar on top. Increase the oven temperature to 200°C / 400°F / Gas 6 and return the pork to the oven for 20 minutes or until glazed and golden. Remove the pork to a warm plate and set aside to rest for at least 20 minutes.

To make the tsatziki place the beetroot in a bowl with the apple, Greek yoghurt, garlic, red wine vinegar, olive oil and horseradish. Mix well to combine, then cover with cling film and chill until needed. This will keep for up to 24 hours.

To serve, place the rocket in a bowl and season to taste, then dress with the red wine vinegar and olive oil. Mix lightly to combine. Carve the rested pork into slices and arrange on warmed serving plates with some of the roasted onion rings. Add the beetroot tsatziki to each one with mounds of the rocket salad and some onions from the tray. Serve with a large bowl of roasted potatoes, if required.

PEPPERED DUCK BREAST, GLAZED RED ONIONS AND CHAMP

This is a quick dinner but with a comfort level of a slow-cooked dish. The juices of the onion and duck combine with the mash to give you that heart-warming feeling. If you can't get hold of small duck breasts simply use two larger ones and increase the cooking time.

Serves 4

4 small Barbary duck breasts
about 50 ml / 2 fl oz olive oil
about 3 tablespoons red wine vinegar
1 teaspoon cracked black pepper
6 large potatoes, quartered
4 red onions, quartered
splash red wine (optional)
1 tablespoon redcurrant jelly
pinch ground ginger
2 sprigs fresh thyme, finely chopped
good knob butter
splash cream
100 ml / 3 1/2 fl oz milk
1 bunch spring onions, trimmed and finely chopped
salt and freshly ground black pepper

A couple of hours before cooking, trim the excess fat from the duck breasts and then score the fat with a sharp knife. Arrange on a plate and drizzle both sides with a splash of the olive oil and a tablespoon of the red wine vinegar. Season with the cracked black pepper and cover with cling film. Chill until needed – this will allow the flavours to develop.

Cook the potatoes in a covered pan of boiling salted water for 15-20 minutes until tender.

To prepare the glazed red onions, heat a little of the olive oil in a heavy-based pan. Tip in the red onions and sauté for 3-4 minutes until beginning to colour around the edges. Reduce the heat and continue to cook for 5 minutes until well softened. Add the red wine, if using with the remaining two tablespoons of the red wine vinegar, the redcurrant jelly, ginger and thyme, and simmer for another 5 minutes or so until all the liquid has reduced to a light syrup, stirring once or twice. Season to taste and keep warm.

Heat a heavy-based frying pan with the rest of the olive oil. Pat the duck breasts dry with kitchen paper and add to the pan, skin side down, over a high heat. Cook for 3 minutes, then turn over and reduce the heat. Cook for another 3-4 minutes depending on the thickness of the duck. Season with salt and transfer to a plate. Leave to rest in a warm place for 10 minutes.

When the potatoes are cooked drain them well and then return to the pan with the lid on. Leave to steam dry for a few minutes in their own heat, then mash well. Beat in the butter, cream, milk and spring onions and then season to taste. Return to a low heat to keep warm.

Strain any juices from the duck into the glazed onions, stirring to combine, then heat the glazed onions through. Carve each duck breast into a couple of slices and drain on kitchen paper. Spoon the champ on to warmed serving plates and spoon over the glazed red onions. Arrange the duck on top and finish with the remaining juices from the glazed onions to serve.

Mashed potato is not a science.

ROASTED MONKFISH, BRAISED LETTUCE, TARRAGON AND RED ONION CREAM

I love cooking monkfish on the bone. Like roasting a chicken, the flavour that's imparted when cooking it whole is tremendous. It's definitely more moist and very easy to eat. This cream sauce was used first with a whole poached salmon I cooked at home for a crowd and is served cold.

Serves 4

150 ml / ¼ pint cream

2 tablespoons crème fraîche

⅓ chicken stock cube, diluted in a tiny bit of boiling water

pinch sugar

1 tablespoon white wine vinegar

1½ teaspoons Dijon mustard

1 small red onion, finely diced

2 tablespoons chopped fresh tarragon

1 tablespoon rinsed capers

good splash sunflower oil

2 tablespoons plain flour

1½ teaspoons paprika

4 x 250 g / 9 oz monkfish tails, well trimmed but with bones intact

good knob butter

1 head iceberg lettuce, carefully broken into large leaves

salt and freshly ground black pepper

lemon wedges, to garnish

pilaff rice, to serve (see page 31)

To make the tarragon and red onion cream, bring the cream, crème fraîche and chicken stock to the boil in a pan. Add the sugar, white wine vinegar and mustard, stirring to combine. Remove from the heat and leave to cool completely, then add the red onion, tarragon and capers and season to taste. Transfer to a bowl and cover with cling film. Chill until needed. This will last up to 24 hours in the fridge.

Bring a pan of salted water to the boil and heat a large, heavy-based frying pan with the sunflower oil. Mix together the flour, paprika and seasoning in a bowl and then tip on to a flat plate. Use to dust the monkfish fillets, shaking off any excess.

When the oil is almost smoking, carefully add the monkfish to the pan. Reduce the heat to medium and cook for 3 minutes on each of the fatter sides and 2 minutes each on the other sides, adjusting the heat if necessary so it doesn't burn. Bear in mind that because the fish is quite sturdy and on the bone it will take a little longer for the heat to penetrate into the centre of the fish. To check whether or not it's cooked, insert a knife into the thicker end of the fish by the bone.

When the monkfish is cooked, strain off the excess oil and add the butter to the pan. Allow it to foam and coat the fish. Season to taste and leave to rest for a couple of minutes while you blanch the lettuce.

Plunge the lettuce into the boiling salted water and prod under the water with some tongs. As soon as you have achieved this, drain well on kitchen paper and season to taste, making sure there is no excess water. Divide the lettuce among warmed serving plates. Place the monkfish beside it and spoon the tarragon and red onion cream over it . Garnish with the lemon wedges and serve with the pilaff rice.

GOOSEBERRY CRISP

We ate in Alice Waters' eponymous restaurant on Shattuck Avenue in Berkley, San Francisco, on our honeymoon more years ago than I care to remember – it's been going since the 70s and she's a legend in culinary circles. If I last for 30 years in the business I will most certainly be shipped out to a home for the bewildered, so 'respect'. This gorgeous recipe is adapted from the *Chez Panisse Café Cookbook*.

Serves 4

600 g / 1 lb 5 oz gooseberries, topped and tailed
100 g / 4 oz sugar
3 tablespoons plain flour

For the Topping

75 g / 3 oz shelled walnuts or blanched almonds
150 g / 5 oz plain flour
3 tablespoons light muscovado sugar
2 tablespoons sugar
pinch ground ginger
pinch salt
6 tablespoons softened butter
vanilla ice cream or lightly whipped cream, to serve

Preheat the oven to 190°C / 375°F / Gas 5. To make the topping, place the walnuts or almonds in a baking tin and toast for about 5 minutes or until golden brown. Leave until cool enough to handle and then roughly chop. Place the flour in a large bowl with both of the sugars, the ginger and salt, then mix well to combine. Add the butter and rub it in until the mixture resembles fine crumbs. Stir in the chopped nuts. This topping should come together when squeezed. Set aside.

Place the gooseberries in a large bowl with the sugar, then sprinkle over the flour and mix gently to combine. Tip into an ovenproof dish just large enough to hold the fruit and create a mound in the centre. Spoon over the topping and press down lightly. Place the dish on a baking sheet to catch any juices and bake for 40-50 minutes until the topping is dark golden brown and the juices have thickened slightly. Serve warm straight from the dish on to warmed serving plates with the vanilla ice cream or whipped cream.

Here's another thought on gooseberries – poached gooseberries with elderflower and yoghurt. Place equal quantities of sugar and water into a pan – the amount depends on the amount of gooseberries you have – use your judgement on this. Bring to a gentle simmer and pop in two to three elderflower sprigs and two fresh bay leaves, if you have them. Throw in your gooseberries and cook over a gentle heat for 15 minutes. Remove from the heat and leave to cool. Take out the elderflower and bay leaves and serve in bowls with a dollop of good natural yoghurt. This will keep in the fridge for up to one week.

I know the lady loves Milk Tray but one could get killed!

CHOCOLATE RIPPLE SEMIFREDDO WITH AMARETTO CARAMEL

Believe it or not, the first time I ate semifreddo was only last year. Now I've been around the block in the eating stakes so this is most remiss of me. Anyway I've resolved to make up for lost time and will make and scoff as much of it as possible in the future – now that's what I call ambition. A semifreddo is not quite an ice cream – what you end up with is a block of smooth, soft, semi-frozen flavoured cream that's so easy to make, you simply have to try it. The thing is to master the technique and add whatever flavouring you want after that.

Serves 4

150 g / 5 oz plain chocolate (at least 55 per cent cocoa solids)
1 egg
4 egg yolks
100 g / 4 oz caster sugar
300 ml / 1/2 pint cream

For the Amaretto Caramel

125 g / 4 1/2 oz caster sugar
2 tablespoons Amaretto liqueur

Line a 900 g / 2 lb loaf tin with cling film. Melt the chocolate in a bowl over a pan of gently simmering water and set aside to cool a little. Place the egg and egg yolks in a separate bowl with the caster sugar and a tablespoon of water. Beat over a pan of simmering water for 8-10 minutes until the mixture is pale and thickened – you must persevere with this. In another bowl, whip the cream until thick peaks have formed, then fold into the egg mixture. Finally fold in the melted chocolate in a thin steam, folding slowly – don't incorporate it fully as it should be uneven and nicely marbled. Pour into the loaf tin, cover with cling film and place in the freezer for 4-5 hours until just set (see intro.).

To make the Amaretto caramel, place the caster sugar in a heavy-based pan with 75 ml / 3 fl oz of water over a moderate heat. Slowly bring to the boil, taking care that the sugar is dissolved before it boils. Simmer until the mixture turns a rich golden brown, then immediately remove from heat.

Taking great care, as the caramel may spit, add the Amaretto liqueur, return the pan to the heat and stir until smooth – this may be done well in advance and chilled.

To serve, turn out the semifreddo on to a suitably sized plate and carefully remove the cling film. Drizzle with the caramel just before serving. Once out of the freezer this can melt fairly quickly so perhaps plate it earlier and return it to the freezer until you are ready to roll. Serve straight to the table for the maximum effect.

TIP

You can use rum, whiskey or brandy in the caramel if you don't have Amaretto.

The Staff.

JUNE

I was born on 29 June on the feast of St Peter and St Paul. I've no complaints really, either name would have done. After all, I could have been born on the feast of St Gertrude and the religious connotations may have outweighed the everyday practicalities for my parents.

I am getting a bit edgier with each passing birthday but everyone will concede that the big 40 is something for everyone to reflect upon. I set myself goals at the turn of every milestone with varying degrees of success. Drink a little less; take more exercise; regain my svelte figure – some hope. Naturally, I hope for the business to continue to strengthen. Thankfully the season in Dungarvan has extended as more people visit the area. After all, there is no point in having all this ambition to cook wonderful food if you are scratching around for people to eat it. The money needs to be coming in to pay the staff without whom, I have no hesitation in saying, we are nothing. I know it's a bit of a cliché at this stage but it has taken me a long time to learn what to leave off the plate and not put items on just simply because they are available.

Look at the wonderful bunch of ingredients in season this month. I challenge anyone not to be able to make something spectacular by just combining a few of these. Oh yes – fine for you, you might say, big fancy pants chef; what about us poor buggers coming home knackered after a hard slog all day?

I know it's a bit daunting to think you have to start peeling and chopping when you get home, having left work in a hurry to pick up the kids from crèche. Good shopping ingredients is the key, as good ingredients don't need to be mucked about with.

It irks me to see the local chippers full of kids clutching their fivers to get whatever they want. All the chippers do deals aimed at teenagers, thereby fostering an ambivalence towards good healthy food. It strikes me that most of the fussiest eaters are the fattest. Don't get me wrong – the chipper has its place. There is nothing I would rather after a couple of pints – on occasion. Be brave, shop well. It will be cheaper and healthier in the long run and infinitely more satisfying.

WHAT'S IN SEASON IN JUNE

FRUIT cooking apples, cherries, gooseberries, rhubarb and strawberries VEGETABLES asparagus, broad beans, broccoli, carrots, celery, courgettes, cucumber, fennel, herbs, lettuce, peas, new potatoes, radishes, rocket, sorrel, spinach, spring onions and turnips (new season) FISH bass, black sole, brown trout, clams, crab, young salmon, haddock, hake, lobster, monkfish, mussels, prawns, red mullet, salmon, sea trout and shrimps POULTRY duckling MEAT new season lamb.

SUMMER VEGETABLE BROTH WITH HERBY DUMPLINGS

This is a very open-minded soup that's perfect as a starter or light lunch – delicate, light and bursting with freshness. If you have some roast chicken leftovers, make a stock to use as a base. The same goes for ham. Beef juices from a roast would be fine topped up with some chicken stock cube. The vegetable mixture will do the rest. The herby dumplings give a punchy heartiness that's hard to beat.

Serves 4 as a starter or light lunch

large knob butter
1 small onion, finely chopped
4 spring onions, finely chopped
1 carrot, finely chopped
2 small courgettes, finely chopped
handful broad beans, peeled or fresh podded peas
1 small garlic clove, finely chopped
a few asparagus spears, finely chopped (optional)
1 litre / 1 3/4 pints chicken, ham or light beef stock (see recipe intro.)

For the Dumplings

40 g / 1 1/2 oz butter, at room temperature
1 egg, beaten
50 g / 2 oz fresh white breadcrumbs
2 tablespoons chopped fresh mixed herbs, such as rosemary, thyme and/or sage
salt and freshly ground black pepper
fresh bay leaves to garnish

To make the dumplings, beat the butter in a bowl with a wooden spoon. Add the egg, beating all the time, and then add a pinch of salt, the breadcrumbs and herbs until they are all well blended. Form into little balls about the size of a Malteser and set aside until ready to use.

Heat a large, heavy-based pan over a low heat. Add the butter and once it has stopped foaming, sweat the onion for about 5 minutes until softened and translucent, stirring occasionally. Add the spring onions, carrot, courgettes, broad beans or peas, garlic and asparagus, if using. Sweat for another 2 minutes, stirring.

Pour the stock into the vegetable mixture and bring to the boil rapidly. Add the herb dumplings, reduce the heat and simmer for 5 minutes until the dumplings are cooked through but all the vegetables have retained their colour and texture. Season to taste and ladle into heatproof serving glasses or warmed serving bowls. Garnish with the bay leaves and serve at once.

SPRING ONION OMELETTE WITH GRAVADLAX AND MUSTARD DRESSING

This omelette is similar to an Italian frittata. It is simple and elegant, and a very good example of what can be achieved when you buy wisely. It should be left soft and luxurious, with a creamy yielding texture that complements the gravadlax perfectly.

Serves 4 as a starter or light lunch

3 tablespoons olive oil
small knob butter
4 spring onions, trimmed and thinly sliced
8 eggs
good glug cream
1 tablespoon crème fraîche
dash freshly squeezed lemon juice
1 1/2 teaspoons Dijon mustard
150 g / 5 oz gravadlax (marinated and cured smoked salmon)
1 tablespoon rinsed capers (optional)
salt and freshly ground black pepper

Preheat the grill to high and heat a large non-stick frying pan. Add one tablespoon of the olive oil and the butter and once the butter has stopped foaming tip in the spring onions. Sauté gently for 1 minute.

Meanwhile, break the eggs into a large bowl and add the cream. Season to taste and whisk until well combined.

Pour the egg mixture into the sautéed spring onions and cook for another 2 minutes, stirring gently with the back of a fork.

Place the omelette directly under the grill for 2-3 minutes until the top is lightly golden but the middle is still a little soft.

Meanwhile, make the crème fraîche dressing. Place the crème fraîche in a bowl with the remaining olive oil, lemon juice and the Dijon mustard. Season to taste and whisk until well combined. Add a tablespoon of hot water to the dressing if you think it is a little thick. Set aside.

Put a flat plate or baking sheet on top of the frying pan and carefully invert the omelette. Cut into four slices and transfer to serving plates with a fish slice. Drape the gravadlax over the top and spoon around the crème fraîche dressing, then garnish with the capers, if liked, before serving.

CRAB TOES WITH ROCKET, LEMON AND GINGER

I wanted to show you a dish where lettuce can be used for more than just a traditional garnish or on the side for your lunch. This is a perfectly simple lunch dish. Just be sure to use the best crab toes you can find. You can use frozen but when you defrost make sure to give them a gentle squeeze to eliminate the water.

Serves 4 as a starter or light lunch

juice of 1 lemon
good pinch freshly grated root ginger
1 tablespoon caster sugar
100 ml / 3½ fl oz natural yoghurt
24 crab toes, thawed if frozen (see recipe intro.)
two good handfuls rocket
1 bunch radishes, trimmed and cut into quarters
salt and freshly ground black pepper

Place the lemon juice in a pan with the ginger and sugar. Bring to the boil, stirring until the sugar has dissolved, then remove from the heat and leave to cool. Transfer to a bowl, whisk in the yoghurt and set aside.

Place the crab toes in a large bowl and add the rocket and radishes. Season to taste and using a large metal spoon, gently fold together. Divide among serving plates and drizzle the yoghurt dressing on top to serve.

The first time I ever saw crab, I was in Helvick Head with my Auntie Peggy, the nun, who was home from England on holidays. The eerie, monstrous claws scared the bejasus out of me but I quickly got over that one once I got my gob round them. I recently went over to Auntie Peggy's sixtieth jubilee celebrations. For all you sceptics out there, I would heartily recommend a shindig in a convent. Boy, do you get treated well.

One thing that really gets on my goat is when virtually everything in a particular restaurant is placed 'on a bed of lettuce'. This is an obvious plate-filling scam that bears no relation to good cooking.

CHORIZO, NEW POTATO, EGG AND LITTLE GEM SALAD

This is a slightly simplified version of a very popular warm salad we put on in the summer time. I always keep chorizo oil to use whenever possible. Its sublime spiciness gives an extra dimension to anything it's mixed with, in this case some softly fried eggs. The origins of this salad, as you might have guessed, lie in Spain, the current leader in gastronomic exploration.

Serves 4 as a starter or light lunch

12 small new potatoes, halved
dash sunflower oil
175 g / 6 oz raw chorizo, sliced
4 eggs
4 little gem lettuces, separated into leaves
1 red onion, sliced into rings
8 piquillo peppers or 2 roasted red peppers, drained and cut into quarters (from a jar)

For the Sherry Dressing

1 small garlic clove, crushed
1/2 teaspoon sifted icing sugar
3 salted anchovies (optional)
1 tablespoon sherry vinegar
splash amontillado sherry (optional)
50 ml / 2 fl oz light olive oil
Maldon sea salt and freshly ground black pepper

To make the sherry dressing, place the garlic, icing sugar, anchovies, if using, sherry vinegar, and amontillado sherry, if using, in a bowl with the olive oil. Season to taste and whiz with a hand blender until emulsified. Pour into a sterilised jar and store in the fridge for up to 1 week – any longer and the garlic will begin to taste rancid.

Place the potatoes in a pan of boiling salted water and simmer for 8-10 minutes until tender. Drain and keep warm.

Heat the sunflower oil in a non-stick frying pan and quickly fry the chorizo so it releases its oil, then transfer to a bowl with a slotted spoon and set aside.

Reheat the remaining oil in the pan and break in the eggs. Cook gently for a couple of minutes, spooning a little of the oil over the yolks so they become semi-soft. Remove from the heat.

Divide the little gem lettuce leaves among four serving bowls and scatter over the chorizo, potatoes, onion rings and peppers. Drizzle over enough of the sherry vinegar dressing to just coat the salad. Season to taste and place a fried egg on top of each one to serve.

COURGETTE RISOTTO WITH KNOCKALARA CHEESE, TOMATO AND BASIL

This is one of the classic flavour combinations. If you can't get good plum tomatoes, use canned instead – infinitely better than those unripe, cardboard, pretend tomatoes.

Serves 4 as a starter or light lunch

1.5 litres / 2¹/2 pints chicken stock (from a stock cube is fine)

dash olive oil

large knob butter

1 onion, finely chopped

400 g / 14 oz Arborio rice (risotto)

glass dry white wine

450 g / 1 lb ripe plum tomatoes, seeded and chopped or a 400 g / 14 oz can chopped tomatoes

2 courgettes, thinly sliced

handful fresh basil leaves, torn, plus extra leaves to garnish

150 g / 5 oz Knockalara cheese (soft sheep's cheese)

salt and freshly ground black pepper

Pour the stock into a pan and bring to a gentle simmer. Heat a separate large, heavy-based pan. Add the olive oil and then tip in a knob of the butter. Once the butter has stopped foaming, add the onion and sauté over a gentle heat for 3 minutes. Add the rice and cook for a further two minutes, making sure every grain is coated with the oil and butter. Pour in the wine and allow to cook, stirring occasionally, until it is completely absorbed. Add the tomatoes and cook for another minute.

Stir a ladleful of stock into the rice mixture and allow it to be almost completely absorbed before adding another ladleful of stock, stirring constantly. Continue to cook for another 15-20 minutes until the rice is *al dente* – tender with a slight bite. Season to taste.

Meanwhile, bring a large pan of salted water to the boil. Add the courgettes and blanch for 1 minute, then drain and plunge into iced water. Once they have cooled down, tip on to kitchen paper and allow to dry completely.

Remove the cooked risotto from the heat and stir in the blanched courgettes and torn basil to warm through. Divide among warmed wide-rimmed serving bowls and break up the Knockalara cheese to scatter on top. Garnish with some fresh basil leaves to serve.

I love being close to the land, but not too close, mind you. The aesthetics of it all really appeal to me while chugging along in my jeep. I admit to being a little precious with all the pulling and dragging involved but in the kitchen I am transformed into Rambo Flynn, immersed in culinary detritus and bristling with concentration.

BAKED SEAFOOD WITH PERNOD CREAM, PENNE, FENNEL & SUNBLUSH TOMATOES

As a chef, my mission in life is to be as 'un-cheffy' as possible: simplify my food yet eat well. This is a prime example – you can mix around the fish, just make sure they are cut the same size, otherwise some will be undercooked and some over. The juices released from the fish mingle with the cream and Pernod to form a stunning sauce – dig into this and go to heaven!

Serves 4

225 g / 8 oz penne pasta
olive oil, for brushing
2 good handfuls mussels, cleaned
handful clams, cleaned (optional)
handful whole Dublin Bay prawns
some small cracked crab claws
4 small red mullet, scaled and cleaned
200 g / 7 oz monkfish tail, cut into even-sized chunks
1 fennel bulb, trimmed, halved and thinly sliced
handful sunblush tomatoes
3 garlic cloves, thinly sliced
pared rind of $1/2$ orange
good glug Pernod
200 ml / 7 fl oz cream
salt and freshly ground black pepper
lemon wedges, to garnish
crusty bread, to serve

Preheat the oven to 220°C / 450°F / Gas 7. Plunge the penne into a large pan of boiling salted water, stir once and cook for about 8 minutes until almost but not quite *al dente* as it will finish cooking in the oven.

Drain and quickly refresh under cold running water to prevent further cooking. Set aside.

Take a deep roasting tin and criss-cross 2 x 76 cm / 30 in lengths of tin foil, making sure that there are no gaps where liquid might leak out. Brush the base and overlapping sides all over with olive oil. Arrange half the cooked penne with the seafood, fish, fennel, sunblush tomatoes, garlic and pared orange rind. Season lightly and arrange another layer on top with the remaining ingredients. Drizzle over the Pernod and cream and then bring up the sides of the foil together, folding over to secure. Make sure there are no holes in the foil that would allow any of the steam to escape.

Place the roasting tin directly on your strongest hob for 2 minutes, until the foil has begun to puff up, and then sit it in a large roasting tin. Transfer to the oven and bake for 10-15 minutes until the parcel has puffed up and the contents are cooked through. To serve, bring the tin directly to the table and get your guests to hover around as you unfold the tin foil, savour the smell and ladle into warmed serving bowls. Garnish with lemon wedges and have a basket of crusty bread to hand for all those delicious juices.

STRAWBERRY YOGHURT MERINGUES

I adore meringues in any form. These mini versions will not only look great but the yoghurt will temper the sweetness of the meringue. The strawberries have to be tip top, otherwise this simple exquisite dessert won't work. To bite into a sun-ripened strawberry is one of life's great pleasures. Leave the winter ones on the shelf and surprise your loved one with a glass of champagne or Cava with a ruddy strawberry dancing among the bubbles and secreting its aroma and who knows, you might get lucky.

Serves 4

4 egg whites
225 g / 8 oz caster sugar
6 tablespoons thick natural yoghurt
drop vanilla extract
225 g / 8 oz strawberries, hulled and quartered

Preheat the oven to 150°C / 300°F / Gas 2. Line two large baking sheets with non-stick baking parchment paper and set aside. To make the meringue, whisk the egg whites in a large clean bowl until stiff peaks have formed. Whisk in the sugar, a third at a time, whisking well after each addition until stiff and very shiny.

Divide the meringue into four blobs that are well spaced apart on the lined baking sheets – the more rough and ready the shapes the better. Using the back of a spoon, hollow out a rough well in the centre of each one. Bake for 45-60 minutes or until crisp but not coloured. Transfer to a wire rack and leave to cool completely.

Place the yoghurt in a bowl with the vanilla extract and stir to combine, then fold in the strawberries. Pile into the centre of the meringues and arrange on serving plates to serve.

I know it's a month away yet but the Dungarvan Show is something I always make a point of attending. Amidst all the tractors, show jumping, tug of wars and hi-tech milking parlours is the craft tent, frequented by precious few men. I'm always there and no, I am not a big Jessie, for it takes a rare type of man, confident in his machismo I'll have you know, to look at the flower arrangements, apple tarts, cakes, prize vegetables, jams and chutneys. For some inexplicable reason, I'm extremely popular with, ahem, shall we say the more mature ladies. Naturally I'm delighted to have any form of popularity with the opposite sex but upon reflection, it is a tad frustrating for a fellow that had to work way too hard for their younger counterparts' attention in every disco in Munster in my single days. Is there some sort of inbuilt switch they hit at fifty or do they just want to mother me? Well, they can't seriously want to feed me. Anyway I love that day out, the tent and especially the cakes …

Tarts don't last five minutes in our house. I'm the guilty one, of course. One slice straightaway with a cup of tea. It's so nice, I can't stop thinking about it. Just another little one, it won't hurt. Twenty minutes or so later again I just happen to be in the kitchen and there it is, teasing me, 'eat me, you know you want to'. Before I know it three-quarters of it is gone. What will I do with the evidence? … I could throw it away but that would be wrong. Yes, you've guessed it. By now my own twisted logic tells me to eat it. I'll be good tomorrow, I tell myself. Of course, I am never good, so there you have it. What a piglet!

CUSTARD TART WITH POACHED RHUBARB AND GINGER

This classic custard tart, when made well, is one of the finest foods known to man. Paired with fruit, it becomes a classy version of rhubarb and custard. Choose the reddest rhubarb you can find or feel free to experiment with the fruit.

Serves 6–8

500 ml / 16 fl oz cream
8 egg yolks
75 g / 3 oz caster sugar
$1/2$ teaspoon ground ginger

For the Poached Rhubarb

550 g / $1^1/4$ lb rhubarb, cut into 3 cm / $1^1/4$ in lengths
125 g / $4^1/2$ oz caster sugar
drop vanilla extract
pinch ground ginger

For the Pastry

225 g / 8 oz plain flour, plus extra for dusting
pinch salt
150 g / 5 oz butter, diced and chilled
75 g / 3 oz icing sugar, sifted
1 egg
1 egg yolk

To make the pastry, sift the flour and salt together into a bowl. Rub in the butter until you have fine breadcrumbs. Stir in the icing sugar and then bind with the egg and egg yolk. Shape into a ball and chill for at least 30 minutes before using. You'll only need half for this recipe but the rest can be frozen for a later date.

To make the poached rhubarb, place the rhubarb in a large roasting tin with the sugar, vanilla extract and ground ginger. Mix well to combine and then cover with tin foil. Bake for 30 minutes until completely tender but still holding its shape. Remove from the oven and carefully drain the juice into a small pan. Reduce by two-thirds and then leave to cool completely before folding back into the poached rhubarb to make a 'jammy' but not broken up compôte.

Preheat the oven to 190°C / 375°F / Gas 5. Roll out the rested pastry on a lightly floured surface as thinly as possible and use it to line a loose-bottomed 20 cm / 8 in fluted flan tin that is about 4 cm / $1^1/2$ in deep – any excess can be left hanging over the sides and trimmed once baked. Chill for 10 minutes to allow the pastry to rest.

Reduce the oven temperature to 180°C / 350°F / Gas 4. Line the pastry case with a circle of non-stick parchment paper that is first crumpled to make it easier to handle. Fill with baking beans or dried pulses and bake for about 15 minutes until the case looks 'set', but not coloured. Carefully remove the paper and baking beans, and allow to cool.

Reduce the oven temperature to 130°C / 250°F / Gas $1/2$. To make the custard filling, place the cream in a pan and bring to the boil. Meanwhile, put the egg yolks, sugar and ground ginger in a bowl and whisk until light and fluffy. Pour in the hot cream, whisking continuously, then pass through a sieve into a clean bowl and skim off any remaining froth from the surface. Pour into the baked pastry case and bake for 30-35 minutes until the custard has just set but still has a slight wobble in the middle. Remove from the oven and leave to cool for about 5 minutes, then trim away any excess pastry. Leave to cool completely at room temperature. To serve, cut into slices and arrange on serving plates with a spoonful of the rhubarb compôte.

I started to scream as I held on for dear life.

JULY

Ah yes, by now we are in the thick of it. The restaurant operating at full tilt is tiring and challenging, yet an exhilarating time. I love the buzz of a busy restaurant. It takes on a life of its own. I seem to have more staff than ever swarming about the place. Restaurants are so labour intensive sometimes I wish for a simpler, quieter life without so many people to be responsible for but this life is like a drug and if you want to do it right you need the people. I seem to be incessantly calling on the boys in the kitchen to clean this, wipe that. The mornings are hectic, with deliveries to be checked and recorded. These days even dead meat gets its temperature probed more than I ever have in my life time. There are empty boxes, endless wrapping, bottles and jars to be recycled. Then you need to sweep the floor. How can you work like that, I constantly moan. There is so much work to do the boys don't see it; three to four times a morning it is swept but I still seem to moan. I get tired of my own voice but they all do their best, ploughing through the jobs. 12 o'clock comes and yet another sweep, mop and wiping down of the work surfaces. A relative calm descends, waiting for the first customers. Suddenly it's off out of the traps again.

We are threatening to go to the Galway races this year if we can get away. We probably won't be able to but as you may already be aware I know absolutely nothing about horse racing. In this part of the country this is tantamount to being a weirdo. Everyone is horse mad around here. I have been in company, totally bewildered with the jargon, soft going, covering, hands and heels ... I smile stupidly and pretend I know what's going on, although I know they have me sussed by now.

There are racehorses at the bottom of our drive; two sets of stables on the way into town and stable lads ride out past our front door every day. Our friends are deeply involved. One of them is always trying to get me to buy a leg of a horse, although he must have labelled me tight as his demands have now scaled down to offering me a bit of a dog instead. Eunice, a good friend, rang the other day, hugely excited as their mare had given birth to a colt foal. I tried to be as excited as I could but she knew I just didn't understand how big a deal it was. I want to go to the races but I could be on top of the Gold Cup winner and still someone would have to explain the seriousness of it all to me. Mingling and have a good time with friends is much more appealing.

My one and only time on a horse was on an old mare called ESB. My friends had stables and being aware of my nervousness, they

Three or four times it's swept, but still I seem to moan.

produced the quietest, most gentle animal for my apprehensive, untrained rear. To cut a long story short, I was no budding Pat Eddery. The horse bolted straight for an open gate that led to the road, panic set in; and I started to scream as I held on for dear life. People were waving frantically, trying to divert the horse. Thankfully someone managed to close the gate and grab the reins. The last gallop probably killed ESB. It certainly killed my enthusiasm for riding.

If we do mange to make it to the Galway races I will round up a gang and have a picnic. Nothing too flash for I don't want people throwing me those *'who do you think YOU are'* looks while queuing for their burgers and chips. From where I am standing now on the dizzy precipice of 40 I could go two ways. The quiet refinement of a picnic basket is the obvious choice of someone who is aware of the imminence of middle age or the devil may care attitude of a cool box – packed with beer, as in my rock festival youth. It's also useful as a platform for a better vantage point until your girlfriend (now wife) looks up at you and pleads to take your place for a minute. You step down, knowingly manipulated, never to reach the dizzy heights of high altitude for the remainder of the day. So this begs the question, is your proverbial cup of life half empty or half full? Therefore, I will divide the options into two.

WHAT'S IN SEASON IN JULY

FRUIT blackberries, blackcurrants, cherries, gooseberries, loganberries, peaches, raspberries, redcurrants, strawberries and white currants **VEGETABLES** globe artichokes, beans (broad, French and runner), beetroot, broccoli, carrots, celery, chard, courgettes, cucumber, herbs, kohlrabi, leeks, lettuce, peas, new potatoes, radishes, rocket, sorrel, spinach, spring onions, tomatoes and turnips (new season) **FISH** bass, black sole, brown trout, grey mullet, haddock, halibut, lemon sole, lobster, mackerel, prawns, salmon, sea trout, shrimps and swordfish **POULTRY** duckling.

FOR THE COOL BOX

Weighty decisions have to be made here, ie, the proximity and time involved in getting to the bar. This will affect the contents greatly. If queuing doesn't bother you, then pack it with food. The over-anxious amongst you may want to pack a little beer in case of emergencies or an attack of sheer laziness.

SANDWICHES ... good because they are easy to pack, easy to eat and don't involve cutlery.

Some suggestions:

Crab mayonnaise with avocado on brown

Roast lamb with hummus and cucumber in pitta

Brie with smoked ham in a baguette with your favourite chutney

Sausage, mustard and onion marmalade on white

Bacon, mozzarella and tomato with pesto in a bap

Cambazola with sliced plums on walnut bread

Tayto crisps with loads of butter on white

Parma ham and goats' cheese with ciabatta and figs

Chicken tikka in small naan breads

Roast beef and English mustard with my own nectarine chutney (sorry, but if are passing ...!)

Rice, bean and pasta salads are possible too. Avoid the leafy types, as they are a bit girly and not at all durable. These can be stored for best effect in Chinese take-away containers. Remember space is crucial, so lean against the car. **Eat and ponder the odds.**

SALAD SUGGESTIONS

Tabouleh – cous cous, mint, parsley, tomatoes, peppers and raisins

Three bean – your favourite beans, crispy bacon and mustard vinaigrette

Tomato and mozzarella – chunky tomatoes and mozzarella with red onions, olives and basil

Egg and tuna mayonnaise with spring onions for bite

Orzo pasta with smoked chicken, baby spinach and horseradish cream

Penne with garlic sausage and spicy tomato sauce

Potato and smoked duck, with hazelnut oil and sherry vinegar

Asian noodle salad, peanut butter, coconut milk, coriander, soy sauce and chillies blended together and poured over cooked noodles, then garnish with chopped peanuts

Poached salmon, pickled cucumber and new potatoes

Roast lamb through cucumber raita with tomatoes and onion

Not to forget, you'll need something sweet – buy some buns!

FOR A PICNIC BASKET

One snazzy hamper, one rug, wine or champagne. Sit down, relax, look aloof and ignore the hoi polloi.

Suggestions

Plate of charcuterie – sliced smoked duck, chicken, Parma ham and paté with some Mickey Mouse luncheon meat if there are children.

Baguette, butter, relish and gherkins.

Paté de foie gras, if you want to really impress.

Smoked salmon with cucumber, crème fraîche and brown bread

Grilled lamb cutlets served cold, with a creamy butter bean and white truffle dip

Asparagus wrapped in Parma ham with Boilie cheese

Cold lobster mayonnaise, green salad and new potatoes

Dressed crab with guacamole cream and tortilla chips

Prawns in lemon and lime mayonnaise with little gems

Carpaccio of beef – love it or loathe it, a good one is delicious

Cold leg of lamb, scattered with roasted aubergine, tomato, onion, feta cheese and olives

Strawberries and cream with pink champagne

PAPPA AL POMODORO WITH PRAWNS TOMATO AND BREAD SOUP

This is not really a soup as we know it, but one of those ingenious ideas from Italy for using up ingredients that were hanging around and weren't going to be thrown away. This may be served hot, warm or cold on a fine summer's day. Lobster tails would also be fantastic with this.

Serves 4 as a starter or light lunch

1 large day-old white loaf or focaccia
100 ml / 3¹/₂ fl oz extra virgin olive oil, plus extra for drizzling
1 large red onion, finely chopped
1 celery stick, finely chopped
1 large carrot, finely chopped
2 bay leaves
1 garlic clove, finely chopped
5 large tomatoes, peeled (very ripe and juicy)
12 fresh large Dublin Bay prawns
2 fresh basil sprigs
Maldon sea salt and freshly ground white pepper

Cut the crusts off the bread and cut into slices, then cut each slice into 5 cm / 2 in squares. Set aside. Heat half the oil in a deep pan over a medium to high heat. Add the onion, celery, carrot, bay leaves and garlic and cook for about 10 minutes until completely tender and almost sauce like. Add the whole tomatoes, whisking constantly and continue to cook for another 5-10 minutes until the tomatoes are soft and have dissolved into the rest of the vegetables. Pour in 900 ml / 1¹/₂ pints of water and bring to the boil.

Add the bread to the pan, then reduce the heat and simmer for 10 minutes, stirring occasionally. Remove the bay leaves and add a teaspoon of salt and a pinch of the ground white pepper. Whisk until the bread has completely broken down and the soup is smooth. Keep warm.

Meanwhile, remove the shells from the prawns and season to taste. Heat the remaining oil in a large heavy-based frying pan over a medium to high heat. Add the prawns and cook for 2 minutes, or until tender, tossing occasionally.

To serve, spread some of the soup on to the centre of warmed wide-rimmed serving bowls. Add the sautéed prawns and spoon any remaining juices from the pan on top. Drizzle each plate with a little more oil. Tear the basil leaves and scatter on top. Season with pepper and away you go.

There is a little story from Romagna which goes as follows. There was once a priest who was always poking his nose into other people's affairs, not with malice, just simple nosiness. The parishioners who were nevertheless very fond of him nicknamed him Don Pomodoro (Don Tomato) because, like the tomato, he was into everything.

Ann Franco Taruschio, *Leaves from the Walnut Tree*

KNOCKALARA CHEESE WITH FRESH PEACHES FRENCH BEANS AND OLIVES

This sings of the summer. Knockalara is a favourite of mine. You will notice it cropping up elsewhere in this book. It is a soft and creamy sheep's cheese from Cappoquin in Waterford Knockalara and a fresh peach eat wonderfully together. To that I've added some olives, French beans, a little red onion and a punchy citrusy dressing. Use feta cheese as a good alternative.

Serves 4 as a starter or light lunch

two handfuls French beans, trimmed

12 black olives (your favourite)

1 small red onion, thinly sliced into rings

generous pinch chopped fresh mint

2 ripe peaches, stoned and sliced

4 tablespoons extra virgin olive oil

juice of 1 lime

juice of 1/2 lemon

150 g / 5 oz Knockalara cheese, cut into 1 cm / 1/2 in cubes (soft sheep's cheese)

salt and freshly ground black pepper

Plunge the French beans into the boiling salted water and cook for about 3-4 minutes. I don't like beans too crunchy – the flavour is much better when they have just a little bite.

Drain off the beans and run them under the cold tap, or as we do in the restaurant plunge them into a large bowl of iced water, to arrest the cooking and promote the colour but you need a bit of spare ice for this. If in doubt put the ice in your gin and tonics. Place in a bowl and add the olives, red onion, mint and peaches.

To make the dressing, place the olive oil in a separate bowl with the lime and lemon juice. Season to taste and whisk until well combined.

Turn the salad mixture very gently and add the Knockalara cheese. Spoon on to serving plates and drizzle the dressing on top to serve.

SUMMER VEGETABLE AND POTATO SALAD

I use this either as a salad on its own or with some lovely chorizo or Parma ham. It's fantastic under a piece of grilled fish with some aïoli on the side. You will notice I follow the restaurant-style practice of blanching my vegetables, then refreshing them in iced water. This will allow you to control the cooking time and preserve the wonderful colours which are essential to this fabulously vibrant dish.

Serves 4 as a starter or light lunch

16 baby new potatoes, peeled and halved
1 green and 1 yellow courgette, sliced
1 small leek, trimmed and sliced
10 asparagus spears, trimmed
4 shallots, finely chopped
2 tablespoons snipped fresh chives
10 cherry tomatoes, halved

For the Apple and Lemon Vinaigrette

2 tablespoons caster sugar
1 tablespoon freshly squeezed lemon juice
25 ml / 1 fl oz white wine vinegar
pinch English mustard powder
75 ml / 3 fl oz peanut or sunflower oil
2 tablespoons olive oil
25 ml / 1 fl oz apple juice (good quality –
Crinnaghtaun, if possible)
salt and freshly ground black pepper

To make the apple and lemon vinaigrette, place the sugar in a small pan with the lemon juice and white wine vinegar. Bring to the boil and cook until the sugar has dissolved but the liquid has not reduced. Remove from the heat. Whisk in the mustard powder, oils and apple juice. Season with plenty of black pepper and pour into a sterilised jar. This will keep in the fridge for 3-4 weeks.

Place the potatoes in a pan and just cover with water, then bring to the boil. Reduce the heat, cover and simmer for 10-12 minutes or until tender.

Meanwhile, bring a large pan of salted water to the boil. Blanch the courgettes for a minute or so and then plunge into a large bowl of iced water. Repeat with the leek and asparagus spears. Once the vegetables have completely cooled down, drain into a colander and then tip on to kitchen paper to dry completely.

Drain the potatoes and tip into a large bowl, then stir in a little of the vinaigrette so the flavour can be absorbed. Fold in the shallots, season to taste and allow to cool completely.

Add the blanched vegetables to the cooled potato mixture with the chives and cherry tomatoes, and then gently fold together using a large metal spoon. Season to taste and drizzle in enough of the remaining vinaigrette to just coat but not soak the salad – you may have a little leftover. Divide among serving plates and serve at once.

GRILLED LAMBS LIVER WITH CUMIN APRICOTS AND TABBOULEH

I wanted to serve lambs' liver in an interesting summery way. As much as I love serving it with mash, colcannon or champ, that's for the chillier months when we need every bit of comfort we can get. The tabbouleh is made from bulgar wheat, available from health food shops and well worth looking for. If you cannot find it substitute with cous cous.

Serves 4

splash olive oil
675 g / 1 1/2 lb lambs liver, cut into 1 cm / 1/2 in slices
pinch ground cumin
splash red wine vinegar
pinch light muscovado sugar

For the Tabbouleh

75 g / 3 oz bulgar wheat
handful chopped fresh flat-leaf parsley
1 red onion, finely diced
2 garlic cloves, crushed
2 plum tomatoes, seeded and diced
pinch chopped fresh mint
50 ml / 2 fl oz extra virgin olive oil
50 ml / 2 fl oz fresh lemon juice
salt and freshly ground black pepper

To make the tabbouleh, soak the bulgar wheat overnight in a bowl with 250 ml / 9 fl oz of water. The next day, drain off any excess water and stir in the parsley, red onion, garlic, plum tomatoes, mint, olive oil and lemon juice. Season to taste and mix lightly to combine. Cover with cling film and set aside at room temperature to allow the flavours to mingle.

Meanwhile, heat a heavy-based frying pan with the olive oil until almost smoking. Place the liver carefully in the pan, then season and sprinkle over the cumin in an even layer – you may have to do this in batches depending on the size of your pan. Cook for 1 1/2 minutes or so, then turn over and cook for another minute until just tender but still pink in the middle.

Transfer the cooked liver to warmed serving plates and keep warm. Return the pan to the heat and add the vinegar and sugar, scraping the bottom of the pan to remove any sediment, and then allow to bubble down for a few minutes into a sauce. Spoon over the liver and serve with the tabbouleh alongside.

Interested in a filly's leg, Paul?

RIB EYE STEAK & SOFT POLENTA, WITH SPRING ONIONS & DESMOND CHEESE

There are two key things about this dish: firstly, there is nothing finer than a well hung, well marbled rib eye – a steak cut from the eye of a rib roast. Sure, it's a little tougher than oh so boring fillet, but the flavour. It's a real man's cut this. Secondly, I used to hate polenta until I ate some amazing stuff in the Botanical restaurant in Melbourne last year. As soft as baby food but throbbing with just the right amounts of white truffle oil and Parmesan, finished with a softly poached egg nestling in the centre. This was food for no ordinary baby; this was truly heir to the throne stuff. So I revised my opinion of polenta. I know I said I didn't want this to become a world food book, but I didn't want it to be dominated by the spud so I will say that you could incorporate these flavours into a mash or a risotto if you are not fully convinced by the merits of polenta. By the way, Desmond is a Parmesan-like cheese made in west Cork by the ultra-interesting Bill Hogan – if you find it hard to get use Parmesan or if you like blue a little Crozier, Cashel Blue or Gorgonzola.

Serves 4

1 litre / 1³/4 pints milk
1 small onion, roughly chopped
4 garlic cloves, halved
few sprigs fresh thyme
2 bay leaves
100 g / 4 oz instant polenta
4 x 225-275 g / 8-10 oz rib eye steaks
a little olive oil
75 g / 3 oz Desmond cheese (see recipe intro.)
1 tablespoon softened butter
1 bunch spring onions, trimmed and finely chopped
salt and freshly ground black pepper

Place the milk, onion, garlic and herbs in a pan and bring to almost boiling point. Place the polenta in a large heavy-based pan and strain in the infused milk, whisking continuously until blended. Continue to stir the polenta mixture over a moderate heat until it comes to the boil, then reduce the heat to very low and cook for 3-4 minutes or according to the instructions on the packet, stirring often. Leave to stand for two minutes.

Meanwhile, take a large frying pan or even better a large griddle pan and heat well until almost smoking. Brush your steaks with the olive oil and season, then place on the pan and cook for 3-4 minutes on each side, moving them once on the same side if you have a griddle pan to get that nice criss-cross effect. Naturally, cook the steaks the way you like them yourselves but I would strongly suggest no more than medium. Remove from the pan and place on a large plate. Leave to rest in a warm place for no less than 10 minutes while you are putting the finishing touches to the polenta.

Fold the Desmond cheese into the cooked polenta with the butter and spring onions – the residual heat will cook the spring onions. Season to taste. Divide the rested steaks among warmed serving plates and place a dollop of polenta alongside each one. Pour any steak juices from the plate on top to serve.

'Sure, leave it in the oven until the fire brigade comes'
– now there's a man who likes his steak well done.

BUTTER-POACHED WILD SALMON WITH PARSLEY CRUSHED POTATOES

I'm fed up with using farmed salmon. I'm certainly turning into a purist as I get older. Farmed salmon is becoming one of the cheapest fish around, and maybe that's a good thing. I suppose people will eat more fish if it's cheaper but I'd rather eat the good stuff less often. June and July, to be precise, have my fill and let it alone until I'm next allowed to eat it without harming the stocks. I'm not usually so PC, firmly believing that a healthy dose of rebelliousness is essential to make one's character more interesting. Anyhow, I poach my salmon in a little emulsion made with fish stock, white wine and butter. It's really easy and imparts the fish with an amazing buttery flavour. I then use the poaching liquid to make a parsley sauce that I crush with new potatoes and roasted hazelnuts. Yum.

Serves 4

16 new potatoes
about 20 skinned hazelnuts
300 ml / $^1/_2$ pint fish or light chicken stock
100 ml / 3$^1/_2$ fl oz white wine or apple juice
75g / 3 oz butter, diced
2 shallots, sliced
1 bay leaf
4 x 150 g / 5 oz skinless salmon fillets, boned
good handful fresh flat-leaf parsley leaves
a splash of cream (if you feel bold)
$^1/_2$ lemon, pips removed
4 eggs
salt and freshly ground white pepper
lemon leaves to garnish

Preheat the oven 180°C / 350°F / Gas 4. Place the new potatoes in a covered pan of boiling salted water and cook for 12-15 minutes or until tender. Drain well and keep warm. Roast the hazelnuts in a small baking tin for 4-5 minutes until evenly coloured, tossing occasionally. Leave to cool and reserve a handful to garnish, then crush the remainder with a pestle and mortar.

Place the fish or chicken stock in a wide, deepish pan that will fit the salmon fillets comfortably. Add the white wine or apple juice and bring to the boil. Whisk in the butter over a medium heat and add the shallots and bay leaf. Do not boil but keep the liquid at 85°-90°C / 170°-180°F which is just below boiling point but with no bubbles. Season to taste, then submerge your fish in the liquor. If it doesn't cover the fish don't worry and just turn the fish once during cooking. Poach for 6-7 minutes until the fish starts to feel firm to the touch and loses that flabby plumpness it possesses. I like to leave salmon just a little rare in the middle but if you like it more well done then leave it a minute longer.

Remove the cooked salmon fillets with a fish slice and arrange on a plate. Season to taste, then cover with another plate or piece of foil to keep the heat in – it will continue to cook a little here so be careful. Bring your cooking liquid to the boil and reduce by one-third as quickly as possible. Remove the bay leaf and throw in the parsley. Cook on a moderate heat for 2-3 minutes and then whiz with a hand blender until reasonably smoothish. At this point you could add a little cream, season to taste and add a little lemon juice to taste.

Meanwhile, place the eggs in a pan of boiling water and simmer gently for 6 minutes, then drain and quickly run under the cold tap to prevent them from cooking further. Peel away the shells and set aside until needed.

Lightly crush the cooked new potatoes with a fork and then add in enough sauce to just bind the potatoes but not make them sloppy, reserving the remainder. Throw in the ground hazelnuts and again season to taste. Divide the crushed potatoes on to warmed serving plates. Uncover the salmon and squeeze a little lemon juice on top then arrange on the plates. Spoon

SWEET & SOUR MACKEREL WITH CARROTS, RED ONION AND CHICKPEAS

We put this on in the restaurant recently and it was a big hit, both with the customers and staff. The colours were so vibrant and the flavours so fresh I couldn't take it off for the mackerel season. There is a little bit of knife work here so stick on a bit of music, do a Floyd – Keith that is – if it's not too early in the day and have a glass of wine. Enjoy it. I usually serve this with new potatoes and a salad.

Serves 4

4 large mackerel filleted and pin boned
150 ml / ¼ pint olive oil (good quality)
2 red onions, thinly sliced
1 carrot, thinly sliced
4 cm / 1½ in knob fresh ginger, peeled and finely chopped or grated
1 cinnamon stick
½ teaspoon coriander seeds
50 ml / 2 fl oz white wine vinegar
good pinch sugar
400 g / 14 oz can chickpeas, rinsed and drained
a little fresh lemon juice
salt and freshly ground black pepper
boiled new potatoes and lightly dressed salad, to serve (optional)

TIP

If you don't have a non-stick frying pan, lightly flour the mackerel before cooking.

Heat a non-stick frying pan until just smoking. Season the mackerel. Add two tablespoons of oil to the heated pan and heat again. Fry the mackerel, skin-side down, for about 2 minutes, then flip them over and cook for another 2 minutes. Transfer to a deep serving dish, skin side up, and allow to cool.

Wipe out the pan and heat half the remaining oil. Gently sauté the red onions and carrot with the ginger, cinnamon and coriander seeds for about 5 minutes or until softened. Add the vinegar, sugar and remaining oil. Bring to the boil and season to taste. Add the chickpeas and allow to warm through, then spoon the mixture over the mackerel fillets and pop into the fridge to serve later that day, or even better the following day. I like to serve it at room temperature but it is also delicious lightly warmed.

To serve, either warm up in a preheated oven at 180°C / 350°F / Gas 4 covered with foil for 15–20 minutes or remove from the fridge and allow to come back to room temperature. Arrange the mackerel on serving plates with some of the chickpea mixture and serve with new potatoes and a salad, if you like.

CHERRY SUMMER PUDDING WITH WHITE CHOCOLATE FLAKES

Everybody loves a summer pudding. I've made this one with fresh cherries. I've added some white chocolate shavings on top for texture and a bit of extra luxury.

Serves 8

2 tablespoons sugar
1 cinnamon stick
800 g / 1³/₄ lb stoned cherries
about 8 slices day-old white bread, crusts removed
1 small bar white chocolate (good quality)
crème fraîche or whipped cream, to serve

Place the sugar in a pan with 500 ml / 16 fl oz of water and the cinnamon stick. Bring to the boil, then reduce the heat and simmer gently until the sugar has dissolved. Add the cherries and poach gently for about 10 minutes or until they start to soften. Remove from the heat and leave to cool a little.

Cut a circle from one slice of bread to fit into the base of a 1.2 litre / 2 pint pudding basin, then cut the rest of the bread into 5 cm / 2 in strips and quickly dip into the cherry juice until lightly soaked. Use most of it to line the sides, in a slightly overlapping layer (reserving enough to make a lid).

Carefully spoon the poached cherries into the lined pudding basin, taking care not to dislodge the bread – Reserve a few of the cherries to decorate. Return the pan to the heat and reduce the juice by half – this will take about 5 minutes. Remove and discard the cinnamon stick.

Meanwhile, cut the remaining bread to fit entirely over the fruit but don't put it on yet. Stand the pudding basin on a plate and whiz the cherry mixture until

blended with a hand blender. Spoon some of the sauce over the cherries and place the bread lid on top, but do not overfill. Place a saucer or small plate on top so it just sits inside the basin. Chill overnight. Reserve the remaining sauce in a serving jug covered with cling film in the fridge.

To serve, run a knife carefully around the inside of the basin rim, then invert the pudding on to a cold serving plate. Decorate with the reserved cherries and pour some of the remaining sauce on top. The rest can be put on the table. Shave the white chocolate with a vegetable peeler and stand it on top. Bring to the table and cut into slices, then arrange on serving plates with dollops of the crème fraîche or whipped cream.

AUGUST

I love sunny days but I hate the sun. Does that make sense? My nightmare holiday would be grilling myself on a sun lounger in Costa del High Rise, dripping with factor 50, eating dodgy food, waiting for the inevitable sunburn and the thunderous bouts of the trots. I faced a few facts a long time ago: Speedos and me were never going to be bosom buddies, indeed shorts are a little bit scary on me, not being blessed with the best set of legs on the planet. I try to respect other people's sensibilities by wearing them as little as possible. All I ask for is fine bright weather. I get cranky and tired in a lot of heat - not that we have to worry about that in Dungarvan.

The beauty of good weather is the abundance of fine products it produces. Even my herbs at home thrive, and that's saying something, when all I have to do is look at a plant and it dies. I try to do a little entertaining at home, if we can snatch the time, cooking and eating outside. It makes life so much easier, with much less mess. Sipping a beer while barbecuing something snazzy, looking down on the town from our lofty perch in Glenbeg, the to-ing and fro-ing of the tide telling us the hours are passing.

Work churns along; it always seems that the busier we are the better it seems to go. We settle into a busy but exciting routine. A farmers' market has started in the town and it's tremendously exciting: cheeses, olives, sausages, breads, croissants, organic vegetables and apple juice. There's a snazzy cappuccino stall with ready-made pasta sauces to go, and the puttanesca is a blinder. Baby pancakes with maple syrup are made to order while the shoppers discuss the dining options for the rest of the week. Who would have thought a few years ago this would have happened? I hope to God it continues and thrives.

I love to see the multitude of ingredients arrayed in the stalls while I'm shopping. I think of specials: the cherries for a summer pudding, organic and bursting with flavour. I am inclined to linger far too long at the sausage counter, where they have inviting tasting plates for their wares. I always arrive back to the restaurant with my arms full and my head brimming with ideas.

The busier we are the faster the time goes. Once September arrives the kids go back to school, and the restaurant gets quieter then, as parents are broke after the holidays, plus the school books and uniforms. For me, I always look forward to autumn. I start to swap the lighter olive oils to richer sauces to suit the weather. Slowly does it though. I don't want to wish my life away just because I'm bursting to cook root vegetables again.

I am determined picnics will be a regular event this year. I am always threatening to buy one of those fancy picnic baskets you always see in the shops from early spring but, up to now, I've resisted, convinced it will only end up discarded or padded out with an old jumper, its contents removed to accommodate our increasingly grouchy and ungrateful cat on one of her marathon snoozes.

Ah yes, Sunday evening by the Blackwater, a little paté, some ham or perhaps fresh crab mayonnaise while lolling on a rug sipping Gewurtzraminer. I dream of doing these things but don't get to do them as often as I'd like. Last January a friend invited me for a jaunt in his dinghy from Youghal to Cappoquin. He fashioned a barbecue stand on to which he fixed a disposable barbecue and we grilled burgers in the shivering cold while putt-putting along the river. All the while I was eyeing up suitable spots for a dream picnic, vowing to return without the toe-curling weather.

WHAT'S IN SEASON IN AUGUST

FRUIT apricots, bilberries, blackberries, blackcurrants, blueberries, cherries, gooseberries, loganberries, melons, mulberries, plums, raspberries, redcurrants, tayberries, strawberries, watermelon and whitecurrants VEGETABLES globe artichoke, all the beans, beetroot, broccoli, carrots, celery, courgettes, chard, courgettes, cucumber, kohlrabi, leeks, lettuce, marrow, mushrooms, onions, peas, new potatoes, radishes, rocket, shallots, sorrel, spinach, spring onions, tomatoes and turnips FISH black pollock, black sole, crab, grey mullet, haddock, halibut, lobster, prawns, sea bass, shrimps and turbot POULTRY guinea fowl GAME grouse from 12 August.

MARINATED CHERRY TOMATO SALAD WITH BOILIE CHEESE

Marinated cherry tomatoes are useful with salads, with goats' cheese, feta cheese or even warmed and spooned over fish dishes. Try them on crostini, brushed with tapenade for a simple starter.

Serves 4 as a starter or light lunch

225 g / 8 oz cherry tomatoes, halved

1 large onion, halved and thinly sliced

50 ml / 2 fl oz balsamic vinegar

85 ml / 3 fl oz olive oil

50 g / 2 oz capers, well rinsed

2 garlic cloves, crushed

drizzle honey

1 bunch fresh basil

200 g / 7 oz jar Boilie cheese

salt and freshly ground black pepper

Place the cherry tomatoes in a large non-metallic bowl and add the onion, balsamic vinegar, olive oil, capers, garlic and honey. Season to taste and stir well to combine, then cover with cling film and place in a warm place for at least 1 hour so the cherry tomatoes soften slightly and all the flavours are given a chance to infuse. These can also be kept covered in the fridge for two or three days.

When ready to serve, tear the basil leaves and stir into the marinated cherry tomatoes, then place in a snazzy serving bowl. Drain the jar of Boilie cheese and scatter the balls of cheese on top.

I really only use tomatoes from April onwards. It doesn't seem appropriate in the depths of winter. Tinned tomatoes make a fine soup or sauce at any time but fresh tomatoes? I'd feel guilty for defying the seasons!

WATERMELON GAZPACHO

You *have* to try this soup. It's utterly amazing. We buy mini melons and serve the soup in a scooped out half on a bed of crushed ice; a swirl of yoghurt and toasted almonds complete the experience. The quality of the melon is of utmost importance – the riper the better.

Serves 4–6 as a starter or light lunch

1/2 watermelon
1 garlic clove, sliced
1 tablespoon finely chopped fresh root ginger
4 ripe tomatoes, quartered
1 red pepper, seeded and roughly chopped
good pinch chopped fresh coriander
small handful fresh mint leaves
good pinch chopped fresh basil
good glug olive oil
about 1 tablespoon toasted flaked almonds
2 tablespoons natural yoghurt
salt and freshly ground black pepper

Cut the watermelon in half, then scoop out and discard the seeds. Cut up the flesh and place in a food processor or liquidiser with the garlic, ginger, tomatoes, red pepper, herbs and olive oil. Whiz until well blended and then season to taste. Strain through a sieve into a large bowl, then cover with cling film and chill for at least 2 hours or overnight – the colder the better.

Heat a heavy-based frying pan and toast the almonds for 4–5 minutes, tossing occasionally. Tip on to a plate and leave to cool completely. Set aside until needed.

Give the soup a good stir and season to taste. Ladle into chilled serving bowls on a hot day and add a swirl of yoghurt to each one. Scatter over the toasted almonds and serve at once.

A little birdie told me if you dig a small hole in the top of a watermelon and tip in your favourite vodka, bit by bit, until it can absorb no more, then bung it in the fridge for a few hours, it can be a decadently boozy treat – naughty birdie!

SMOKED CHICKEN PASTA SALAD WITH PEAS AND CASHEW NUTS

You can use any pasta you like for this. The idea is that the pasta is dredged with a sort of pea pesto, then served cold with some sliced smoked chicken. I'm using spaghettini, but as I've I said before you could also use tagliolini or angel hair pasta. You could also try adding a little Gorgonzola to the pesto, plus a little water to stop it getting too thick, and substitute the cashews for toasted almonds.

Serves 4 as a starter or light lunch

2 handfuls fresh or frozen peas
good glug olive oil, plus a little extra as necessary
1/2 lemon, pips removed
1 fresh mint sprig
225 g / 8 oz spaghettini
2 smoked chicken breasts
100 g / 4 oz salted toasted cashew nuts
salt and freshly ground black pepper

Bring a large pan of salted water to the boil and throw in the peas, then cook for 2-3 minutes depending on their size. Drain and cool as quickly as you can preferably in a large bowl of iced water, then drain well and tip into a large bowl.

Add a good glug of the olive oil to the peas and squeeze in the lemon juice. Add the mint, season to taste and blitz with a hand blender until smooth, akin to pesto. If the consistency is too thick, add a little more oil. Season to taste, cover with cling film and set aside until ready to use.

Bring another pan of salted water to the boil and add a splash of the olive oil so the pasta won't stick together. Stir once and cook for 6-8 minutes or according to the instructions on the packet. Drain and quickly refresh under cold running water, then drain well again. Tip the pasta into the pea pesto and season to taste. Stir to combine and then transfer to a serving bowl. Shred the smoked chicken on top and scatter over the cashew nuts to serve.

TIP

Don't be tempted to cook a huge amount of pasta as this recipe is for a starter or light lunch. If you want to serve this as a main course, double the pesto recipe, then cook as much pasta as you think you will need and buy extra smoked chicken.

ORIENTAL CRAB RISOTTO

You have to try this. Not only is it easy to make, but it's utterly delicious. I always serve this risotto with my sesame soy dressing, the recipe for which is with the Asian lamb salad (see page 68) as it makes all the difference but if you haven't got the time or inclination, drizzle a little sesame oil and soy sauce on top, along with a good sprinkling of chopped fresh coriander. A little diced pineapple would be fab in here too.

Serves 4

1.5 litres / 2$\frac{1}{2}$ pints chicken stock
good knob butter
1 onion, finely diced
small knob fresh root ginger, peeled and grated
400 g / 14 oz Arborio rice (risotto)
100 g / 4 oz fresh or canned sweetcorn, drained
450 g / 1 lb fresh white crab meat plus a little brown if you have it
1 bunch spring onions, trimmed and finely chopped
finely grated rind and juice of 1 lime
salt and freshly ground black pepper
sesame soy dressing (see recipe page 68) or toasted sesame oil and soy sauce, to serve
chopped fresh coriander, to garnish

Place the chicken stock in a pan and bring to a gentle simmer. Melt the butter in a heavy-based pan and then tip in the onion and ginger. Cook for a few minutes over a low heat until softened but not coloured, stirring occasionally. Add the rice and turn to coat in the butter, making sure every grain is covered and glistening. Add a couple of ladlefuls of stock – this is the secret – and cook slowly until the rice has absorbed all the stock, stirring continuously.

Add another ladleful or two of stock to the pan and continue this process for 15-20 minutes. You must keep stirring it until the rice is *al dente*, tender but with just a little bite. If you are using fresh sweetcorn, cook in a pan of boiling water for 2-3 minutes, then drain and quickly refresh under cold running water. At this point add the crab to the risotto with the spring onions, sweetcorn, lime rind and juice, then season to taste. Turn off the heat and allow to sit for a couple of minutes to allow all the flavours to combine.

Ladle the risotto into warmed serving bowls and drizzle over a little of the sesame soy dressing or use a little sesame oil and soy sauce instead. Finish by scattering the chopped coriander on top to serve.

LAMB CHOPS WITH MUSTARD AND CAPER BUTTER

I love barbecuing at home. I just bought a shiny new garden set to eat my creations off. The secret with barbecuing is not to cook over the flame. Only when the charcoal or wood settles down to a nice even heat should any cooking be attempted. Isn't it amazing that a man won't touch a saucepan for the entire year but is happy to tinker and dabble over the barbecue whilst sucking on a beer? It seems even with a silly apron on, barbecuing doesn't tarnish the masculinity of the butchest of men. This form of cooking really depends on marinating your meat to give maximum flavour. However, if you don't fancy putting these lamb chops on the barbecue, or there simply isn't the weather, try using a griddle pan.

Serves 4

2 tablespoons olive oil

2 garlic cloves, crushed

$1/2$ lemon, pips removed

4 lamb chops

125 g / $4^1/2$ oz butter, at room temperature

$1^1/2$ teaspoons rinsed capers

1 tablespoon Dijon mustard

1 teaspoon honey

pinch chopped fresh flat-leaf parsley

Fof the Spicy Roast Potatoes

5 large waxy potatoes, scrubbed and cut into 2 cm / $3/4$ in dice

good glug sunflower oil

1 onion, finely chopped

1 mild red chilli, seeded and finely chopped

3 tablespoons balsamic vinegar

5 tablespoons tomato ketchup

salt and freshly ground black pepper

crisp green salad, to serve

To make the marinade, place the olive oil in a shallow, non-metallic dish with half of the garlic and a good squeeze of the lemon juice. Season to taste. Whisk until well combined and then add the lamb chops, turning to coat. Cover with cling film and chill for at least 2 hours or overnight if possible.

To make the mustard butter, place the butter in a bowl and add the capers, Dijon mustard, a squeeze of the lemon juice with the honey, parsley and remaining garlic. Season to taste and beat until well blended. Tip the flavoured butter out on to a rectangle of non-stick baking parchment and shape into a roll, twisting the ends to secure. Leave in the fridge for at least 2 hours or again overnight it until firm.

To make the spicy potatoes, preheat the oven to 220°C / 450°F / Gas 7. Place a glug of the oil in a large roasting tin and heat in the oven for a few minutes. Tip in the potatoes and toss to combine, then season to taste and roast for about 20 minutes or until tender.

Arrange the lamb chops on the grill rack over medium coals on a barbecue and cook for 6 minutes on each side until medium rare.

Meanwhile make the spicy sauce for the potatoes. Place the remaining oil in a pan and tip in the onion. Sweat for a few minutes until softened and then add the chilli. Cook for another 2 minutes and then pour in the vinegar. Reduce a little, stirring before adding the tomato ketchup. Whiz with a hand blender until smooth. Season to taste and add to the cooked potatoes, tossing to coat evenly – they are fantastic, hot or cold.

To serve, arrange the lamb chops on warmed serving plates, then cut discs from the mustard butter and lay on top – any remainder can be used another time. Serve with bowls of the spicy roast potatoes and a crisp green salad.

TiP

It is difficult and pointless to make a smaller amount of the mustard butter than is stated in the recipe. However, it freezes brilliantly and could be used with fish, chicken or beef with excellent results.

BAKED BLACK POLLOCK WITH TOMATOES, OLIVES AND GARLIC

I try to champion the lesser-known fish if I ever can. Black pollock is a fine and much underrated fish with firm, succulent flesh. This is a simply prepared oven-to-table preparation with a bit of a wow factor.

Serves 4

4 large potatoes
2 kg / 4¹/₂ lb black pollock, scaled, slashed gutted and
well rinsed (I normally leave the head on)
5 sprigs fresh rosemary
about 16 mixed olives (good quality)
pared rind 1 orange
4 large plum tomatoes, halved
2 bulbs garlic, broken into individual cloves
few good glugs olive oil
splash white wine (optional)
handful fresh white breadcrumbs
pinch sugar
a little chopped fresh parsley
salt and freshly ground black pepper

Preheat the oven to 220°C / 450°F / Gas 7. Place the potatoes in a steamer and cook for 15 minutes until half cooked. Leave until cool enough to handle and then thickly slice. Lay the fish in a roasting tin, season the cavity and push four of the rosemary sprigs inside. Place the sliced potatoes, olives, orange rind, tomatoes and garlic in the tin around the fish and stick small sprigs of the remaining rosemary into the slashes. Slosh about a good bit of olive oil and add the wine, if you have a bottle open, or a splash of water is fine too. Scatter the breadcrumbs over the top and sprinkle the sugar around the fish, then cover with foil and place in the oven for 20 minutes.

Remove the fish from the oven and take off the foil. Sprinkle over the parsley and bake for another 5 minutes until the pollock is just tender. Serve everyone a little fish, some potatoes, tomatoes and olives on to warmed serving plates. Spoon a little juice on top of each one.

TIP

If you cannot find pollock you can use hake or haddock, or if you want to be a real fancy pants try sea bass.

SUMMER BERRY TRIFLE

I wouldn't dream of taking trifle off the menu during the summer. I serve this one in sexy individual glasses that look amazing on the table. Once the right balance of custard, cream, sponge and fruit is achieved there is nothing nicer.

Serves 6-8

250 ml / 9 fl oz cream
1 teaspoon icing sugar, sifted
1 flan sponge (shop-bought or homemade)
225 g / 8 oz mixed berries, such as raspberries, tayberries, blueberries and strawberries, topped and halved

For the Custard

275 ml / 9 fl oz cream
drop vanilla extract
3 egg yolks
$^1/_2$ teaspoon cornflour
25 g / 1 oz caster sugar
chocolate snaps or shavings, to decorate (see tip below)

To make the custard, place the cream in a small pan with the vanilla and bring to scalding point (almost but not quite to the boil). Whisk the egg yolks, cornflour and sugar together in a bowl until well blended and then pour in the hot cream mixture, stirring continuously. Wipe out the pan and then pour back in the custard. Stir over a low heat for 3-4 minutes or until the mixture coats the back of a wooden spoon. Remove from the heat and leave to cool completely.

Place the cream in a bowl with the icing sugar and then whip until you have achieved soft peaks. Break the flan sponge into pieces and put a little into the bottom of each serving glass. Put a couple of spoonfuls of the custard on top to soak through and then scatter over half the berries. Repeat the process, putting more custard on this time to make sure there are no air pockets in the glasses. Spoon the sweetened cream generously on top of the second layer of berries. Decorate with some chocolate snaps or shavings and place in the fridge for a couple of hours before serving, or overnight is fine.

TIP

Use your favourite chocolate for this recipe. If some of your guests don't like dark chocolate there is no point in trying to get them to eat it – if in doubt, use a flake. They always seem to go down well.

Is that a mango in your pocket or are you just pleased to see me?

CHERRY BERRIES

The colour of cherries sends me homing towards them whenever I see them sparkling at me. This recipe is essentially poached cherries served with other berries, a little poaching juice and a dollop of frozen yoghurt on the side – yum.

Serves 4

250 g / 9 oz cherries
100 g / 4 oz sugar
handful strawberries, topped and halved
handful raspberries
a few blueberries
1/2 lime, pips removed
good pinch peeled chopped pistachios (optional)
frozen yoghurt or ice cream, to serve

Remove the stems and stones from the cherries and then crack the stones by crushing them lightly with the bottom of a heavy-based pan. Place the stones in a pan with the stems, the sugar and 250 ml / 9fl oz of water. Bring to the boil over a high heat, then reduce the heat and cook for 5 minutes until syrupy.

Strain the syrup into a bowl and then return to the pan. Add the stoned cherries and cook over a medium heat for 10 minutes until the cherries are quite tender. Remove from the heat and leave to cool completely. Cover with cling film and chill for at least 4 hours but overnight is best.

To serve, stir the mixed berries into the cherries and add a squeeze of lime juice, then divide among serving bowls, drizzling over some of the syrup. Scatter the pistachios on top and serve with a scoop of frozen yoghurt or ice cream on the side.

TIP

I often serve cherries preserved in liqueur (griottines) with roast quail or put them through a stuffing for duck. Cherries preserved in Kirsch can be bought in good food shops, but beware. One mouthful of these could send you over the limit.

So you're the cause of all my hardship.

SEPTEMBER

At the end of last August I went on a day's organic gardening course at my supplier, Tim Yorke's, smallholding near Lismore. Tim originally hails from Stroud in Gloucestershire. Despite all the hard work, he retains a ready willingness to have a good giggle. His easy manner belies a wealth of knowledge that others are keen to lap up. His huge, calloused hands could do with an immersion in a vat of Nivea for twenty years or so. Fiona, his wife, comes from Waterford via England. A trained theatre actress, she looks after the business side of things. I suspect she's a mighty cook in a modest silent way.

The group of would-be gardeners were treated to elevenses of good coffee with chestnut cake. The chestnuts were picked from the trees overlooking the picture postcard cottage that Tim built with those talented hands of his. Later, our lunch comprised of yellow courgette soup, broad bean paste, the tastiest boiled potatoes oozing with melted butter, a tart of rainbow chard, soft cheese and a

grated Italian pastry I've never heard of before but which was a revelation. Our main meal was accompanied by the simplest tomato salad you could imagine, with marmande tomatoes, olive oil, basil and lots of salt and pepper, the flavours left to copulate with stunning results. I said very little but I took it all in. Blackcurrant fool with cinnamon biscuits was served to finish. I tried to decline the dessert but somehow I never seem that assertive when refusing good food.

It was wonderful to see everything in its natural state. Tim had a solution for everything, using natural methods gleaned from years of experience. For example, to eradicate algae bloom in the watercress pool use a few handfuls of barley stalks to counteract the algae. To deter an aggressive little fly that attacks the carrots – construct a 40cm / 16 in fence around the carrots. The fly comes in low and then can't get at the carrots. Commercial growers call him bonkers, but I had never seen tomatoes so red, tasting so intensely tomatoey; the carrots, the beetroot, mizuna, spring onions, broad beans – tasted like concentrated versions of themselves. Their colours, so vivid, made me think they were on a big veggie outing to the carnival in Rio and wanted to look their best in the hope they might pull some sexy Samba baby veg. I left planning my next week's menu. I ordered extra from Tim for the following Tuesday, thinking how could anybody not want to cook when you're surrounded with produce such as this. Cheers Tim.

Tim and Fiona will be at our season's end barbecue in our home this year, a regular feature in the Flynn household. Speaking of barbecues, I want to tell you a little story while I have the time, and before you say it I realise I'm a very lucky man. The finest barbecue I have ever had was high on a mountain overlooking the Chilean lake district, cooked by a local Chilean farming family with wild pigs roaming around, happily rooting for acorns and recently-dropped apples, while being harassed by the children. This heavenly feast was devoured after a morning's white water rafting down a local river. God, I feel like I am talking about another person, but it was me, making a fool of myself, squeezed into the largest wetsuit the instructor could find, while everyone diplomatically suppressed their giggles.

It is true that hunger is the best sauce but this was glorious food and as simple as it comes. Grilled chorizo sausages and whole racks of ribs kindly supplied by the little piggies roaming around giving credence to the maxim, you are what you eat. Apparently these piggies were distinctive not only by their flavour but by the fact that a few pig generations ago, a lusty old boar came down from the highlands and had his wicked way with the ladies, giving rise to a very unique bloodline. There was belly of pork and topside of beef and a host of salads, fresh corn and chilli, tomato and onions and poached wild salmon. The simplest of grub, yet I will never forget it. We played a local throwing game similar to Boules that night. It was great fun, and very sociable, despite the fact we didn't speak Spanish and our hosts didn't speak English. However, the wine helped fuel the conversation whilst doing nothing for my aim. I had to stop after nearly decapitating one of those pigs, so I retired to a warm observation post by the fire. Ah, the memories …

WHAT'S IN SEASON IN SEPTEMBER

FRUIT apples, blackberries, blueberries, crab apples, damsons, elderberries, figs, nectarines, plums and strawberries VEGETABLES artichokes, beans, beetroot, broccoli, carrots, celery, courgettes, chard, chicory, courgettes, cucumber, kohlrabi, leeks, lettuce, marrow, mushrooms, onions, pumpkins, radishes, rocket, shallots, sorrel, spinach, spring onions, sweetcorn, tomatoes, turnips and watercress FISH brown trout, bass, black sole, cod, grey mullet, haddock, halibut, lemon sole, lobster, mussels, prawns, oysters, shrimps and turbot POULTRY guinea fowl GAME grouse, mallard, pigeon, rabbit.

PUMPKIN SOUP WITH WILD RICE

Cooking with pumpkin is fairly new to the Irish. I hear over and over again that aside from Halloween lanterns people are puzzled by these beauties. There are many varieties of pumpkin and squash and to be honest I'm on a bit of a voyage of discovery myself but I promise to let you in on my findings. The wild rice here is optional. You may find it hard to get but it does impart a wonderful nuttiness. I find it's normally stocked in most good health-food stores.

Serves 6-8 as a starter or light lunch

1.5 kg / 3 lb pumpkin
splash olive oil
1 onion, finely chopped
2 garlic cloves, crushed
2 teaspoons ground cumin
good pinch chopped fresh rosemary
1 teaspoon ground cinnamon
1.5 litres / 2$\frac{1}{2}$ pints chicken stock
handful wild rice
3-4 tablespoons crème fraîche (optional)
salt and freshly ground black pepper

Peel the pumpkin and cut in half, then remove the seeds (if you are ambitious you should dry these out for roasting with some spices; wonderful with salads). Cut the pumpkin flesh into large chunks.

Heat a splash of the olive oil in a deepish pan and add the onion and garlic, then fry gently for 3-4 minutes until softened but not coloured, stirring occasionally. Add the cumin, rosemary and cinnamon and fry for another minute.

Add the pumpkin to the onion mixture, stirring to combine, and then pour in the stock. Bring to the boil, then reduce the heat and simmer gently for about 30 minutes until the pumpkin is completely tender.

Meanwhile, place the rice in a pan of unsalted water and bring to the boil, then continue to boil for about 30 minutes or until tender. Drain well and season to taste.

Purée the soup with a hand blender and season to taste. Ladle into warmed serving bowls and add a dollop of the crème fraîche to each one, if liked. Sprinkle over the wild rice and serve at once.

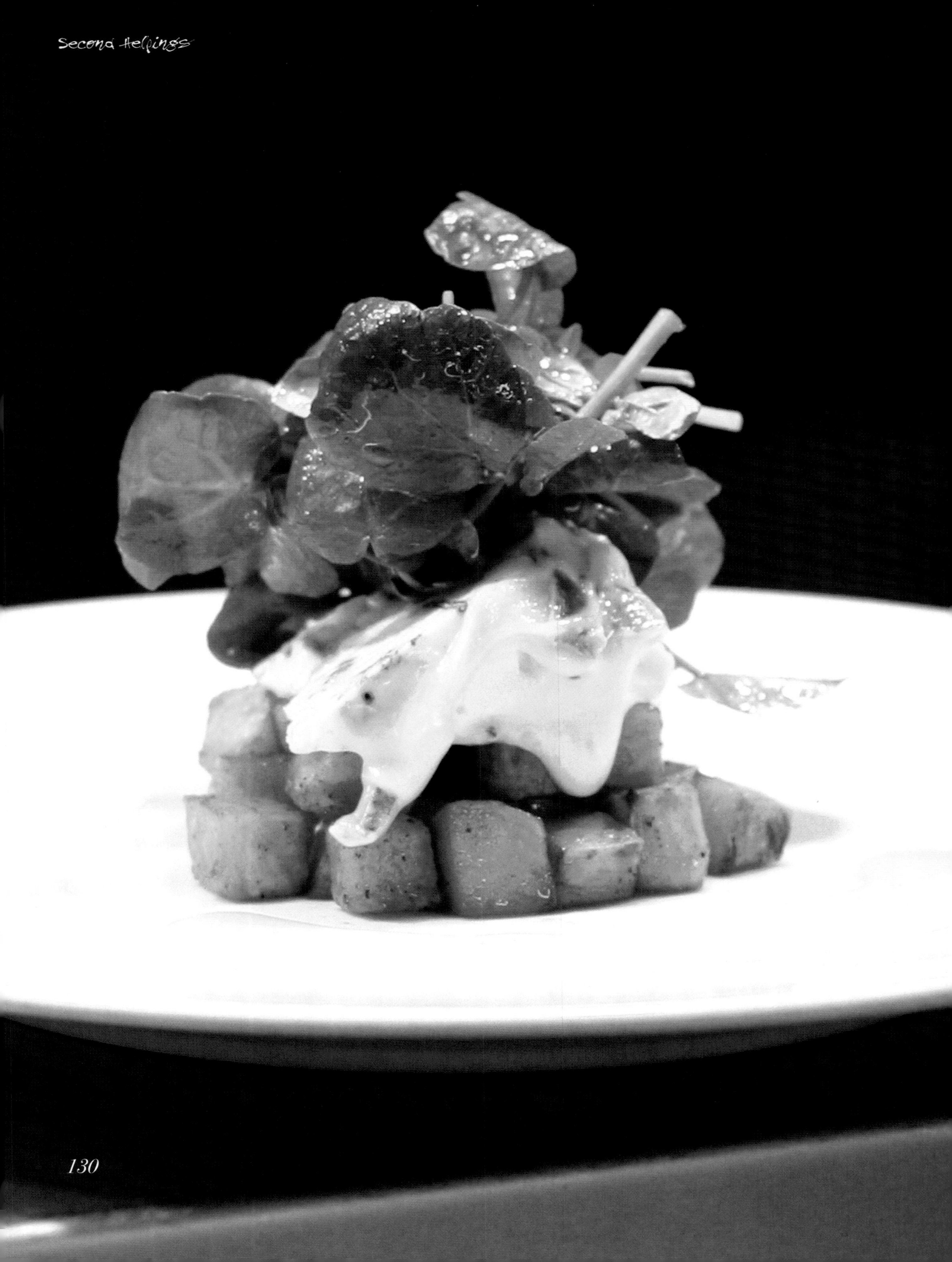

CANDIED TURNIPS WITH CROZIER BLUE AND WATERCRESS

As you may have guessed, I love cheese. I also think that Ireland has a wealth of good cheese so I try not to go abroad for it, without being jingoistic about the whole thing. There are very few ingredients here, and perhaps unusual ones as well, but like I said, it's approaching root vegetable time and I'll do anything to include them in my cooking. If you were brave enough to serve the turnips after dinner, you would certainly get away with this as a cheese course rather than a starter. Crozier blue is a sheep's cheese from County Tipperary. If you cannot find it use Cashel blue or Gorgonzola.

Serves 4 as a starter or cheese course

2 tablespoons sunflower oil

1 small turnip, peeled and diced into 1 cm / ¹/₂ in squares (you'll need a good knife for this as it can be a little tricky)

300 ml / ¹/₂ pint bottle Cidona (carbonated apple drink)

1 tablespoon Demerara sugar

pinch ground allspice

about 225 g / 8 oz ripe Crozier blue cheese (see recipe intro.)

good handful watercress, well picked over

splash olive oil

splash red or white wine vinegar

salt and freshly ground black pepper

Preheat the oven to 200°C / 400°F / Gas 6 and place a shallow roasting tin to heat inside the oven. Add the sunflower oil and the turnip, then shake until well coated and place back into the oven for 5 minutes to colour a little.

Remove the turnip from the oven and pour in the Cidona, then sprinkle over the sugar and allspice, tossing to coat everything evenly. Return to the oven for another 10 minutes until all the liquid has been evaporated and the turnips start to caramelise and get sticky. If you think they need a little more caramelisation give them a couple of more minutes. Remove from the oven and season to taste.

To serve, arrange a little pile of the candied turnips in the centre of each serving plate. Carefully cut the cheese into four even-sized pieces and put on top. The heat of the turnip will soften and melt it. Place the watercress in a bowl and season to taste, then dress with the olive oil and vinegar. Drape this on top of the cheese to serve.

CREAMY MUSHROOMS ON TOAST

These are bad, bad Leroy Brown. They are self indulgent, heavenly and more-ish but they won't do you any favours when its comes to your Weight Watchers weigh in. This is really a teatime dish, although I used to serve a slightly more complicated version on top of the crispy potato cake (see recipe page 69). Use whatever cheese you fancy – Parmesan, Gruyere – but I'm going to use my new favourite, Ester Hill from Offaly. The mushrooms are up to you. If your budget runs to it, try to get wild, even half wild, then half something else, like button or flat cap, although I think there's more flavour in a glass of water than a button mushroom unless you enhance them significantly!

Serves 4 as a starter or light lunch

2 large bread baps (good quality)
good splash olive oil
1 garlic clove, halved
small knob butter
2 handfuls mixed mushrooms, cut so they are more or less the same size (see recipe intro.)
2 shallots, finely chopped
splash ruby red port
a little chicken stock cube, crumbed
300 ml / ½ pint cream
100 g / 4 oz Ester Hill Emmental cheese, grated
½ lemon, pips removed
a little chopped fresh parsley
salt and freshly ground black pepper

Preheat the grill. Cut the baps in two and rub them with a little olive oil and garlic. Arrange on the grill rack and toast them just before you cook your mushrooms, which will be ready in a matter of minutes. Crush the garlic clove and set aside.

Put a large frying pan over the highest heat you can. Add the remaining olive oil and the butter and, when foaming fiercely, throw in the mushrooms with the shallots and reserved crushed garlic. Sauté for a couple of minutes until the juice starts to come from the mushrooms – this will soon disappear.

Add the port to the pan with the chicken stock cube and allow to boil down quickly. Pour in the cream and cook for another 1–2 minutes until the cream starts to coat the mushrooms. Fold in the cheese and allow it to melt, then season to taste and add a squeeze of the lemon juice with the parsley, tossing to combine.

To serve, arrange half a toasted bap on each warmed serving plate and spoon the creamy mushrooms on top.

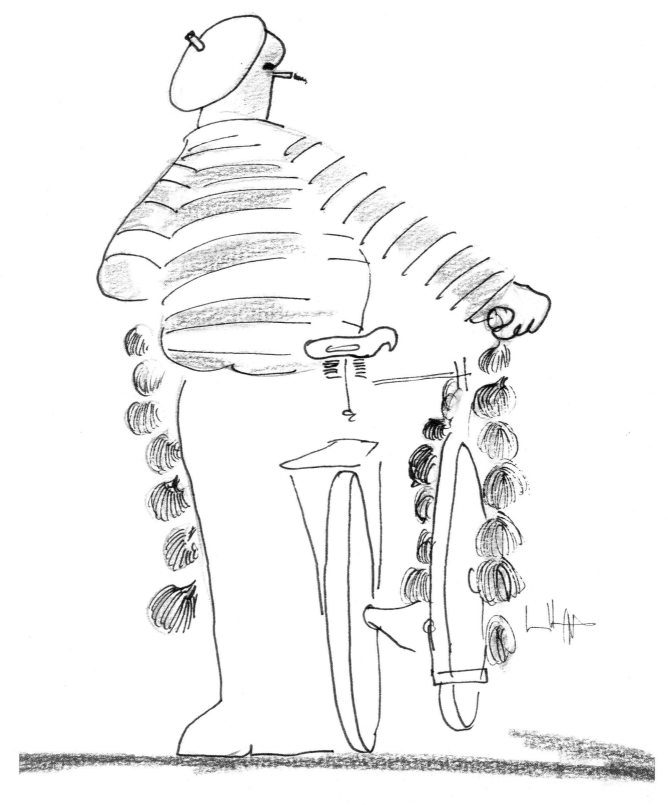

Claude's hauteur dazzled the ladies.

LOBSTER WITH BUTTER BEAN, ORANGE AND FENNEL DRESSING

I'm presuming you're feeling a bit flash and can't resist some lobster irrespective of the price. I usually put my lobster in the freezer for a little while before I cook them. It puts them to sleep and seems a little more humane that way. I'm using a 675 g / 1½ lb lobster that allows for plenty of meat for four people as a starter. If you want more use two lobsters, double the recipe for the beans and serve with boiled or mashed potatoes, or rice or pasta. Indeed the pilaff rice (see recipe page 31) would also be wonderful with it.

Serves 4 as a starter or light lunch

400 g / 14 oz can butter beans, drained and rinsed
juice of 1 orange, plus a little extra if necessary
4 tablespoons natural yoghurt
⅓ cucumber, peeled, seeded and diced
pinch chopped fresh dill
drizzle honey
2 piquillo peppers, drained and diced (from a jar or see below)
pinch sugar
1 teaspoon chopped pickled ginger (optional)
675 g / 1½ lb live lobster (see intro.)
a little olive oil
½ lemon, pips removed
salt and freshly ground black pepper
fresh fennel fronds and whole chives, to garnish

To make the butter bean, orange and fennel dressing, place the butter beans in a bowl and add the orange juice, yoghurt, cucumber, dill, honey, peppers, sugar and pickled ginger, if using. Mix until well combined, adding a little more orange juice if you find the mixture a little thick. Season to taste.

Bring a large pan of salted water to the boil. Immerse your lobster in it, and allow the water to bubble up a little again. This should only take a minute. Remove the pan from the heat and allow the lobster to cool in the water.

When the lobster is cold, take a heavy duty kitchen knife, and starting at the cross on its head, cut right through the shell in as few movements as possible. Try and capture as much of the juice as possible while doing this, and put into a bowl. Add a little olive oil and a squeeze of lemon juice, then season to taste – it doesn't look pretty but this juice tastes divine.

To remove the tail piece from the lobster is easy – the claws take a bit more work. Separate the claws and joints, then crack the claws and the joints to pick out the meat – you'll have to pick the meat out of the joints as best you can but do try to prize the claws out whole. I won't lie, it's a little tricky and requires patience. Divide the lobster meat between serving plates. Spoon the butter bean, orange and fennel dressing into small bowls and set to one side on each plate. Drizzle the reserved olive oil and juice mixture over the lobster meat. Garnish with the fennel fronds and whole chives to serve.

TIP

Piquillo peppers are now readily available in most good supermarkets and delis. I always have a jar in the fridge and tend to use them all the time. However, you could also use half a diced red pepper that has been cooked gently in olive oil.

FRESH HADDOCK IN HAM WITH WARM BLACK MUSHROOMS AND POTATO SALAD

The warm black mushrooms are the key to this dish. You will have to make them ahead of time but once made they keep for weeks in the fridge. I use them in all manner of things, with steak, lamb or through a salad or a pasta dish to give it that extra something.

Serves 4

6 waxy potatoes
3 tablespoons extra virgin olive oil
2 tablespoons red wine vinegar
1 teaspoon Dijon mustard
4 spring onions, trimmed and finely chopped
pinch chopped fresh flat leaf parsley
splash olive oil
4 x 175 g / 6 oz pieces skinless and boneless haddock
4 wide slices or 8 thin slices prosciutto

For the Black Mushrooms

knob butter
2 handfuls tight white button mushrooms, cut into
5 mm / 1/4 in dice
200 ml / 7 fl oz balsamic vinegar
3 tablespoons sunflower oil
a little white truffle oil (optional)
salt and freshly ground black pepper
crème fraîche, to serve (optional)

Cook the potatoes in a pan of simmering salted water for 15-20 minutes until tender but still firm.

Meanwhile, prepare the black mushrooms. Heat a large frying pan and add the butter. Once foaming, tip in the mushrooms and sweat for a few minutes until the juices come out and then evaporate. Add the balsamic vinegar and cook gently for another 10 minutes or so until all the vinegar has been absorbed. Add the sunflower oil to loosen the mixture and season to taste, then stir in the truffle oil, if you are using it. This will make quite a bit more than you need but keeps brilliantly in the fridge (see recipe intro).

To make the dressing, place the extra virgin olive oil, red wine vinegar and mustard in a large bowl. Whisk until well combined and then season to taste. Stir in the spring onions, parsley and two tablespoons of the black mushrooms. Drain the cooked potatoes and cut into slices, then fold them in. Season to taste and cover with tin foil to keep warm.

Heat the olive oil in a large frying pan. Season each piece of haddock with pepper and then wrap in the prosciutto. Add to the pan and cook for 3 minutes on each side until crisp and golden brown. Spoon some of the potato salad on each warmed serving plate and arrange a piece of haddock on top. If you like, serve with a little blob of crème fraîche for extra naughtiness.

Dinner parties can be dodgy. It's important not to try to be too obscure in your choice of food. I fell into this trap some time ago, deciding to do a cassoulet, one of my all-time favourites. Well, what a disaster. My beans were undercooked, my pork overcooked and stringy. I was flustered and embarassed. People were hungry and I had no choice but to give it to them. Most were polite and consoled me but my closest friends proclaimed it rotten and suggested I feed it to the dog. Even he eyed it with deep suspicion.

LAMBS' KIDNEYS, SPICED RICE, CHARD AND ORANGE BUTTER

I spent a long time thinking about this one. At first I was going to give it a Far Eastern twist but then I thought that getting into autumn is when I start putting a more Irish slant on my cooking so I thought of Irish spices. Well, none of them are indigenous, of course, but the spices we would use for a spiced beef, for example. I've put those through the rice – they would certainly go with the earthiness of the kidneys. Chard has a certain vagueness to it that wouldn't compete too much with the flavours and orange comes naturally with these spices. Hey presto, a new dish.

Serves 4

a little sunflower oil
12 lambs' kidneys, cut in half and sinew removed
1 orange
good knob butter
pinch chopped fresh flat-leaf parsley
pinch toasted flaked almonds

For the Spiced Rice

splash sunflower oil
knob butter
1 onion, finely diced
1 teaspoon ground allspice
1 teaspoon ground ginger
$1/2$ teaspoon ground mace
300 g / 11 oz long grain rice, well rinsed
handful raisins
salt and freshly ground black pepper
steamed chard or spinach, to serve

To make the spiced rice, heat a heavy-based pan and add the oil and butter, then tip in the onion and sauté for 3-4 minutes until softened but not coloured. Add the spices with lots of freshly ground black pepper and cook for another minute, then add the rice with 600 ml / 1 pint of boiling water and a pinch of salt. Cover and simmer gently for 15 minutes or until the rice is tender and all the liquid has been absorbed.

Meanwhile, heat a large frying pan with the sunflower oil until it smokes. Carefully add the kidneys and cook for $1^1/2$ minutes on each side. Season to taste and transfer to a warm plate. Grate half the rind from the orange and then squeeze out the juice. Return the pan to the heat and add the orange rind and juice, then whisk the butter into the bubbling juice, making sure all the kidney residue is amalgamated into the sauce. Add the parsley and flaked almonds, swirling to combine, then remove from the heat.

To serve, spoon a heap of the spiced rice on to each warmed serving plate and arrange the kidneys alongside. Spoon over the orange butter sauce and serve with the steamed chard or spinach in a separate serving bowl.

BLACKBERRIES WITH BROWN BREAD AND LEMON CREAM

This is easy – as I'm writing, the blackberries are starting to ripen. They are not ready yet but another two weeks will do it. Then it's going to be a blackberry blitz. If you buy the lemon curd it will certainly remove a little of the work but I will give you the recipe anyway. If you do decide to make it you'll only need two tablespoons of this for this recipe but the remainder will keep for a number of weeks in sterilised jars. It's fantastic spread on to toast or using as a filling with whipped cream for cakes and roulades.

Serves 4

40 g / 1 1/2 oz butter
2 thick slices brown soda bread
2 tablespoons Demerara sugar
225 g / 8 oz blackberries
a little icing sugar
200 ml / 7 fl oz cream

For the Lemon Curd

50 g / 2 oz butter
100 g / 4 oz caster sugar
finely grated rind and juice of 2 lemons
2 eggs and 1 egg yolk, beaten together

Preheat the oven to 220°C / 450°F / Gas 7. To make the lemon curd, melt the butter in a heavy-based pan over a very low heat and then add the sugar, lemon juice and rind, stirring until the sugar has dissolved. Stir in the beaten egg mixture and continue to stir over a gentle heat for 15-20 minutes or until the mixture coats the back of a wooden spoon. Remove from the heat and pour into sterilised jars or a bowl, it will continue to thicken as it cools.

Melt the butter in the microwave or in a small pan. Cut the crusts off the brown soda bread and discard, then crumble the remainder on to a roasting tin and sprinkle over the sugar, mixing with your fingers. Drizzle the melted butter on top and stir until well combined, then place in the oven for 3-4 minutes, stirring once or twice until the crumbs are brown and caramelised – a little care is required here, but the lovely crunchy result is well worth the effort. Remove from the oven and leave to cool completely, then break up any lumps.

Reduce the oven temperature to 180°C / 350°F / Gas 4. Spread out the blackberries in a roasting tin and sieve the icing sugar on top. Bake for 2 minutes until the blackberries start to soften and absorb the sugar. Remove from the oven and leave to cool in the tin.

When ready to serve, place the cream in a bowl with two tablespoons of the lemon curd – the remainder can be used at a later stage (see recipe intro.). Whip until soft peaks have formed and then fold in the caramelised breadcrumbs. Make sure you don't do this too far in advance so that the crumbs remain crunchy.

Divide the cooled blackberries into serving bowls and spoon over any remaining juice. Put a generous dollop of the lemon cream on top to serve.

ROASTED PLUMS WITH CHESTNUT HONEY AND MINE GABHAR

If you cannot find chestnut honey, don't let it bother you. Simply use ordinary honey or even Demerara sugar instead. As long as your plums and cheese are good it will be delicious. Mine Gabhar is one of my favourite cheeses, and is only available for a few months of the year so grab it while you can. It's a slightly tart but creamy goats' cheese that when it is right just melts its way into your heart.

Serves 4

4 ripe plums, halved and stones removed
a little butter
2 tablespoons chestnut honey (see recipe intro)
2 Mine Gabhar cheeses (soft-rinded goat's cheese), cut in half
oat cakes, to serve

Preheat the oven to 200°C / 400°F / Gas 6. Place the plums cut side up in a small roasting tin. Put a small piece of butter on each half and drizzle the chestnut honey generously on top. Bake for 10 minutes until the plum halves are slightly softened and bubbling with the honey. Arrange two halves on each serving plate with a piece of the Mine Gabhar cheese and serve with the oatcakes.

'Sprinkle with sugar and bung in the oven.'

Only for my namesake's stellar performance, it would have been an embarassing thrashing.

OCTOBER

I'm sitting here at home staring out at the rain. It's been raining for some days now and I'm getting fed up. Why, may you wonder? You see, as I write it's the 10th of August and to my mind we deserve just a little bit of sunshine before the nights start closing in on us. It's not much to ask, plus as a recent convert to the great game of hurling, I'm pretty unhappy about Waterford's loss to Kilkenny in the semi-final, only for my namesake's stellar performance it would have been an embarrassing thrashing.

So I'm starting to plan for a week away in Tuscany when the restaurant closes – our last time closing at this time of year. Our guesthouse will be open soon and that will need all our attention. The comings and goings of late-night revellers will be new to us. So, far-flung customers can eat and sleep with us (but not in the biblical sense, you naughty person).

In September, the thoughts of all that lovely food just waiting to be devoured by yours truly will perk up my spirits, together with some heart-warming sunshine, Mind you, there is a plus about the dullness of the damp, as it isn't hard to fast forward my thoughts to what I'd like to cook and eat in October. My olive oil usage will be halved in favour of butter and cream. Comforting dishes are the order of the day – sopping up sauces with some bread or mashing your spuds to catch every residue of juice on the plate. These actions speak of true appreciation of the good. Roll the sleeves up and dig in is my motto.

Root vegetables are the stars of my winter menu. Sometimes I feel like Baldrick of Blackadder because of my obsession with turnips, only I have a slightly better haircut. I love roasting pumpkins and squashes with spices, serving them with smoked duck, chicken or turkey, or letting a velvety cheese sauce wash over them, with the pumpkin all rough, shiny and gloriously inviting. I still serve lamb, by now a flavoursome hogget which I braise patiently with whatever takes my fancy – whether it be the shanks braised in red wine with smokey bacon or the neck fillet turned into a refined Irish stew.

Firm fleshed white fish also stars this month because of the colder waters. Quails and guinea fowl feature, stuffed with chorizo breadcrumbs, raisins and soft onions to be served with lentils and mash – the perfect antidote to a crisp autumnal evening. In fact the way things are going comfort food will be making an early appearance this year.

WHAT'S IN SEASON IN OCTOBER

FRUIT apples, blackberries, blueberries, crab apples, damsons, hazelnuts, mandarins, pears, quinces, sloes and walnuts VEGETABLES beans, beetroot, broccoli, cabbages, carrots, celeriac, chard, chicory, kohlrabi, leeks, lettuce, marrows, mushrooms, onions, parsnips, potatoes, pumpkins, radishes, rocket, shallots, sorrel, spinach, swede, sweetcorn, tomatoes, turnips and watercress FISH bass, black sole, brill, cod, grey mullet, haddock, halibut, mussels, prawns, oysters and shrimps POULTRY duck, goose and guinea fowl MEAT lamb (hogget) GAME grouse, hare, partridge, pheasant, pigeon, quail, rabbit, teal and venison.

OYSTERS IN CIDER CREAM

I have to admit I used to hate oysters until a year ago when my chefs and I ate in the amazing Fishy Fishy café in Kinsale. It was a sort of 'give us a bit of everything Martin' so up came a plateful of oysters in beurre blanc. Now I have to say the boys were all a little queasy from the night before, as Sunday night is their night out. There were a few nervous glances across the table – would the dicky tummies stand up to the oysters? 'Now lads,' I urged, 'I'm going to do it so we all have to do it, we can't be rude.' Well, even the committed oyster abstainees loved them. Of course I've tried both cooked and raw oysters before but each time I practically retch and say never again. Why they were different that day I don't know, but in my new-found enthusiasm I put this dish on the menu.

Serves 4

4 rindless streaky bacon rashers
8 large oysters (preferably native but Pacific are fine too)
150 ml / ¼ pint dry cider (good quality)
150 ml / ¼ pint cream
25 g / 1 oz butter
200 g / 7 oz fresh spinach leaves, thick stalks removed
salt and freshly ground black pepper
brown soda bread, to serve

Preheat the oven to 110°C / 225°F / Gas ¼ and preheat the grill. Arrange the bacon rashers on the grill rack and cook for 3-4 minutes until very crispy, turning once. Allow to cool and then crumble. Set aside.

Scrub the oyster shells, then place one, wrapped in a clean tea towel, on a firm surface with the flattest shell uppermost and the hinge pointing towards you. Gripping the oyster firmly, insert an oyster knife into the gap in the hinge and twist to snap the shells apart. Slide the blade of the knife along the inside of the upper shell to sever the muscle that keeps the shells together. Lift the lid off the top shell, and carefully pour the juices into a small pan. Finally run the knife under the oyster to loosen and remove it from the shell, then place it in a bowl. Repeat until all the oysters are opened, reserving the bottom half of the shells.

Add the cider to the oyster juice in the pan and bring to the boil, then add the oysters and simmer for 30 seconds. Remove with a slotted spoon and set aside. Increase the heat and continue to boil the cider until almost all the liquid has evaporated. Pour in the cream and simmer for another few minutes until thick and reduced by two-thirds.

Meanwhile, melt the butter in a frying pan and heat until foaming. Add the spinach, season to taste and cook for a minute or so, stirring until softened. Remove from the heat and tip into a sieve to drain, then arrange among the bottom oyster shells. Put on a baking sheet and pop into the oven to keep warm.

Return the oysters to the sauce and reheat gently. Season to taste and then place an oyster in each bed of spinach. Coat each one in a little of the sauce. Arrange on serving plates and sprinkle over the crispy bacon. Eat with the brown soda bread.

CORNED BEEF CROQUETTES, MUSTARD AND CUCUMBER DIP

These little babies are based on a traditional Spanish croquette that my chef, Joseph, taught me to make. You can use chicken, ham, turkey, black pudding, chorizo or virtually anything you like in the mix, crab and prawns being especially popular. I wanted to give it an Irish twist so here you are. These are perfect for a party and a great way to use up leftovers. The corned beef is fresh, not the canned variety, so either cook your own (see page 166) or buy it from the deli counter at the supermarket.

Serves 4

500 ml / 16 fl oz milk
100 g / 4 oz butter
1 small onion, finely chopped
200 g / 7 oz plain flour plus two tablespoons
200 g / 7 oz cooked corned beef, diced
2 eggs, beaten with a little milk
200 g / 7 oz toasted dried breadcrumbs
sunflower oil, for deep frying

For the Cucumber Dip

100 ml / 3^1/$_2$ fl oz white wine vinegar
50 g / 2 oz caster sugar
1^1/$_2$ teaspoons wholegrain mustard
^{1}/$_3$ cucumber, peeled, seeded and finely diced
salt and freshly ground black pepper

Place the milk in a small pan and heat until piping hot. Melt the butter in a pan and add the onion, then gently cook for 3-4 minutes until softened and lightly golden. Add 200 g / 7 oz of the flour and continue to cook for another minute over a gentle heat, stirring continuously. Add the heated milk, bit by bit, beating out all of the lumps as you go along. Continue to cook over a low heat for 2-3 minutes until you have achieved a smooth paste.

Add the corned beef to the pan and season to taste, mixing well to combine. Turn the mixture into a shallow roasting tin and leave to cool completely. Cover with cling film and chill for at least 2 hours or overnight is best, until the mixture has firmed up.

To make the cucumber dip, place the white wine vinegar in a small pan with the sugar and bring to the boil, stirring until the sugar has dissolved. Allow to cool a little, then stir in the mustard and cucumber. Transfer to a serving bowl and cover with cling film, then chill until needed.

When ready to serve, preheat the oil to 180°C / 350°F in a deep-fat fryer or deep-sided pan. Place the remaining two tablespoons of the flour on a flat plate and put the egg mixture into a shallow dish, then place the breadcrumbs in a separate dish and line them up. Shape the corned beef mix into small oval balls. Dredge in the flour, and then dip in the egg mixture letting the excess drip off. Finally coat with the breadcrumbs. Deep fry the croquettes for 3-4 minutes or until crisp and golden brown.

To serve, arrange the corned beef croquettes on warmed serving plates and place small bowls of the cucumber dip alongside for dipping.

PUMPKIN AND BLACK PUDDING GNOCCHI

The colour of this is fantastic. It's a big, gutsy dish, heart warming and filling. That's why I love it. If you don't fancy black pudding use smokey bacon and for the people who want to go the whole hog you could make your own gnocchi, otherwise you can buy gnocchi in most decent food shops.

Serves 4

1 kg / 2¼ lb pumpkin
4 garlic cloves, crushed
1 bunch fresh sage
100 ml / 3½ fl oz olive oil
400 ml / 14 fl oz chicken stock
100 g / 4 oz black pudding, cut into the same sized cubes as the gnocchi
450 g / 1 lb prepared gnocchi (see intro.)
50 g / 2 oz Desmond cheese or Parmesan, finely grated
salt and freshly ground black pepper

Preheat the oven to 180°C/350°F/Gas 4. Cut the pumpkin in half and remove the seeds, then score the flesh inside with a knife, being careful not to pierce the skin. Season to taste and smear over the garlic. Remove the sage leaves from the stalks and then chop and reserve the leaves. Scatter the stalks over the pumpkin. Pop into a roasting tin and drizzle over a little of the olive oil. Roast for 30-40 minutes or until the pumpkin is completely tender and can be scraped from the skin with a spoon.

Remove the pumpkin from the oven and leave to cool for 10 minutes. Then using a large spoon, scrape all the pumpkin flesh from the shell, discarding the sage stalks but reserving the leaves, and place in a food processor. Whiz to a fine purée, then pour in the stock through the feeder tube and finally season to taste.

Heat the rest of the olive oil in a large pan and gently fry the black pudding for 2 minutes, tossing occasionally (this will break up eventually so don't worry). Add the reserved sage leaves and cook for another minute, then add the pumpkin purée and bring to the boil. Reduce the heat to its lowest setting and simmer for another 2 minutes until all the flavours are well combined. Season to taste.

Meanwhile, cook the gnocchi in a large pan of boiling salted water for 3-4 minutes or according to the instructions on the packet, then drain and add to the black pudding and pumpkin sauce. Gently fold together and remove from the heat. Ladle into warmed serving bowls and sprinkle the cheese over to serve.

If the grim reaper were to tap me on the shoulder and tell me I had only hours to live, I think I might ask for time for three things: a bit of slap and tickle followed by crispy duck with pancakes and some delicious wine to wash it down. The all-time great is a mixture of crispy duck with sweet cucumber, shredded spring onions, pancakes and hoisin sauce. Then I would say my goodbyes and depart to that great kitchen in the sky — or more likely, the barbecue in the basement.

DUCK, POTATO AND ONION PiE

There's no pastry in this. It's based on Boulangere potatoes, that old French classic of layered potatoes and onion cooked in stock with some herbs and butter. I'm just putting confit of duck in between the layers and serving it with a little buttered cabbage and horseradish cream. If you don't want to make your own you can now buy confit duck legs in good food shops and you'll just need to pop them in the oven to melt away the fat, before forking the meat off the bone. Be sure you reserve the fat for your sauté potatoes at a later time. It keeps forever in the fridge.

Serves 4

400 g / 14 oz potatoes, scrubbed (King Edwards, if possible)

150 g / 5 oz butter

2 onions, thinly sliced

pinch muscovado sugar

splash red or white wine vinegar

2 teaspoons chopped fresh thyme

about 400 ml / 14 fl oz chicken stock

For the Duck Confit

2 duck legs (Barbary, if possible)

1 garlic clove, chopped

1 teaspoon white peppercorns

4 tablespoons coarse sea salt

fat from the duck carcass

peanut oil, if necessary

salt and freshly ground black pepper

buttered cabbage and creamed horseradish to serve

If you are making your own duck confit, first you'll need to marinate the duck legs. Place them in a shallow, non-metallic dish and scatter the garlic, peppercorns and coarse sea salt evenly over the legs. Cover with cling film and place in the fridge for 24 hours to allow the flavours to penetrate the flesh.

Roughly chop the duck fat and place in a heavy-based pan. Add 150 ml / ¼ pint of water and simmer gently for about 2 hours or until the fat begins to look clear. Strain the fat through a fine sieve lined with muslin into a clean pan ready to cook the duck legs.

Rinse the excess spices off the marinated legs, removing the salt as well and pat dry with kitchen paper. Put the legs into the duck fat (if the fat does not completely cover the legs, top it up with the peanut oil). Simmer the duck legs very gently for 1½ hours or until they are very tender and the meat is almost falling from the bone. Remove from the heat and leave to cool in the fat.

Preheat the oven to 180°C / 350°F / Gas 4. Boil the potatoes in a pan of salted water for 10-15 minutes until they are cooked about two-thirds of the way through. Tip into a colander to drain and leave until cool.

Melt one-third of the butter in a heavy-based pan and add the onions. Cook slowly for about 20 minutes or until caramelised, stirring occasionally and then scraping the bottom of the pan all the time to remove the sticky residue when they have turned a deep caramel. Add the sugar and vinegar and then season to taste. Stir well to combine and remove from the heat.

Lightly butter a shallow ovenproof serving dish. Slice the cooled potatoes thinly (use a mandolin if you have one) and arrange half in a layer in the bottom of the dish. Remove the duck confit from the fat and then place in the oven for a couple of minutes to melt any remaining fat. Shred the meat, discarding the skin and bones. Scatter half of the shredded duck confit over half of the caramelised onions and add a sprinkling of the thyme. Season to taste and add a ladleful of stock or so to moisten.

Add the remaining shredded duck confit to the dish, followed by the rest of the caramelised onions, then add the rest of the thyme and season to taste. Add another ladleful of stock and then cover with the rest of the potatoes in an even overlapping layer. Season to taste and dot over the remaining butter. Pour in enough stock to make it moist and bake for 30 minutes or until golden and crunchy. Serve straight on to the table with a separate bowl of buttered cabbage and a dish of the creamed horseradish.

LEMON ROAST CHICKEN WITH GINGER AND PARSNIPS

This is an adaptation of lemon roast chicken from Peter Gordon's *Sugar Club Cookbook*. I had to include it, as it's so deliciously easy, especially if you use a ready jointed chicken. I would serve this with some buttered sprouts and mash.

Serves 4

1.75 kg / 4 lb chicken (preferably organic or free range)
pinch ground ginger
120 ml / 4 fl oz olive oil
1 kg / 2$^{1}/_{4}$ lb parsnips, cut into 2 cm / $^{3}/_{4}$ in dice
1 bunch fresh oregano
2 fresh rosemary sprigs
2 lemons, halved lengthways and thinly sliced
salt and freshly ground black pepper
buttered leeks and mashed potatoes, to serve

Preheat the oven to 220°C / 450°F / Gas 7. To joint the chicken, place the chicken breast side down and with the tip of a knife cut round the two portions of oyster meat (which lie against the backbone). Turn the bird over and cut through the skin where the thigh joins the body. Cut right down between the ball and the socket joint, being careful to keep the oyster meat attached to the leg. Repeat with the other leg.

Separate the thighs from the drumsticks but cutting through at the joints. Trim off the bone end from the drumsticks. Turn the chicken over again, breast side down, and using a poultry shears, cut down firmly through the back into the body cavity between the backbone and one shoulder blade, leaving the wing attached to the breast.

Turn the breast with the wings still attached, skin side up. Remove the wing portions by cutting through at a slight diagonal so that some of the breast is still attached to the wing, then cut each one in half again. You should now have eight portions in total – if all this seems like too much hard work simply buy a packet of chicken joints!

Heat a large frying pan. Season the chicken joints lightly and sprinkle over the ground ginger. Add a little of the oil to the heated pan and use to brown the chicken joints all over.

Meanwhile, place the parsnips in a large roasting tin and add the herbs and half the oil. Season to taste and mix well to combine. Arrange the browned leg joints on top and scatter over the lemon slices. Roast for 15 minutes, then add the rest of the chicken joints and drizzle the remaining oil on top. Roast for another 20 minutes or until cooked through and tender – check by piercing the thickest part of the thigh with a skewer. If the juices run clear the chicken is cooked. Serve straight to the table with separate bowls of buttered leeks and mashed potatoes and allow everyone to help themselves.

CRUNCHY CRUMB BRILL WITH MANDARIN BUTTER AND DILL

I'm baking these brill fillets because it's the easiest way to create a fish dish I know. The fish juices seep into the mandarin juice and butter to create a luscious sauce. The crispy crumbs on top of the fish give it texture. Serve with some crisp green vegetables and pilaff rice. If you cannot get brill use hake or cod instead.

Serves 4

50 g / 2 oz butter
4 x 200 g / 7 oz brill fillets, skinned and boned
juice of 4 mandarins
4 tablespoons fresh white breadcrumbs
pinch flaked almonds
pinch rinsed capers
1 tablespoon chopped fresh dill
salt and freshly ground black pepper
steamed broccoli florets and pilaff rice (see page 31)
to serve (optional)

Preheat the oven to 200°C / 400°F / Gas 6. Melt the butter in the microwave or in a small pan. Brush a little of the butter in a small shallow roasting tin. Season the brill fillets and place them in the tin, then drizzle the mandarin juice on top.

Scatter over the breadcrumbs and almonds in an even layer, then drizzle over the rest of the melted butter. Bake for 5-6 minutes or until the breadcrumbs are crisp and golden and the brill is just tender. Transfer the crunchy crumb brill on to warmed serving plates and keep warm.

Place the roasting tin directly on the hob and add a little water with the capers and dill. Whisk to amalgamate this with the juices to form a sauce and spoon around the fish. Serve with the broccoli florets and some pilaff rice, if you like.

Chefs come in all shapes and sizes.

ROASTED COD LEEK AND POTATO SAUCE WITH PICKLED CARROTS

Make this dish in three stages: first the carrots, then the leeks and potatoes, and then finally cook the cod. The potatoes will be practically runny, the sharp crunchiness of the carrots will prove a perfect foil for their richness, and then, of course, the creamy cod marries the two together into something sublime.

Serves 4

6 floury potatoes
1 small leek, trimmed and cut into 1 cm / 1/4 in dice
a little olive oil
4 x 175 g / 6 oz boneless cod fillets, skin on
good knob butter
100 ml / 3 1/2 fl oz milk, plus a little extra if necessary
splash cream
1/2 lemon, pips removed

For the Pickled Carrots

1 1/2 teaspoons coriander seeds
8 large carrots, very thinly sliced (with a mandolin if you have one)
1 tablespoon cracked black pepper
handful raisins
good sprig fresh thyme
300 ml / 1/2 pint olive oil
250 ml / 9 fl oz white wine
100 ml / 3 1/2 fl oz white wine vinegar
pinch sugar
salt and freshly ground black pepper

Preheat the oven to 180°C / 350°F / Gas 4. To make the pickled carrots I'm going to ask you to prepare more than you actually need because they keep for weeks in the fridge once they are covered. Roast the coriander seeds in a small frying pan for a few minutes until aromatic, then tip into a pan with the carrots. Add the cracked black pepper, raisins, thyme, olive oil, wine, vinegar and sugar. Season with a pinch of salt and cover with a circle of non-stick baking parchment paper.

Bring the pan to a very gentle simmer, then stir and replace the parchment paper. Cook for 3-4 minutes until tender, depending on how thick the slices of carrot are. Remove from the heat while the carrots are still crunchy and allow to cool in the pan. Transfer three-quarters of them to a rigid plastic container with a lid to keep for a later dish. Set the remainder aside until ready to use.

To make the leek and potato sauce, cook the potatoes in a covered pan of boiling salted water for 15-20 minutes until tender. Bring a separate pan of water to the boil and blanch the leek for 1-2 minutes until just soft, then refresh under cold running water. Squeeze out the excess water and set aside.

When the potatoes are almost cooked, heat the oil in a large ovenproof frying pan. When almost smoking, add the cod, skin side down, and season to taste. Cook for 3-4 minutes, then turn over, add a small knob of butter and allow to foam. Pop into the oven for another 3-4 minutes until just cooked through and tender.

Meanwhile, drain the potatoes and return to the pan, and then put back on the hob over a low heat for a couple of minutes to dry out. Mash well and beat in the remaining butter with the milk and cream, remembering that it needs to be almost a sauce consistency. If not add a little more milk. Add the blanched leek to the potato sauce and allow to just warm through.

Remove the cod from the oven and squeeze a little lemon over it. Place a pool of the potato and leek sauce on each warmed serving plate and arrange a piece of cod on each one. Put a pile of the pickled carrots along with some of the juice on top and serve at once.

BAKED PEARS WITH GINGERBREAD AND CREAM

You can try this without the gingerbread if you like. It will still be scrumptious but I just think that final flourish lifts it to another crunchy level.

Serves 4

small knob butter

4 large pears (firm but ripe)

300 ml / ½ pint cream

50 g / 2 oz caster sugar

2 drops vanilla extract

pinch ground cinnamon

pinch ground nutmeg

1 teaspoon freshly grated root ginger

4 slices gingerbread, crumbled

sprigs fresh mint to decorate

Preheat the oven to 190°C / 375°F / Gas 5. Lightly butter a large shallow baking dish, or four individual ones. Peel the pears and cut in half lengthways, then carefully remove the cores. Arrange in the buttered dish, cut side down in a single layer.

Mix the cream, sugar, vanilla, cinnamon, nutmeg and root ginger, until well combined. Pour over the pears and then bake for 20 minutes until the pears are almost tender and the cream mixture is well reduced.

Remove the pears from the oven and sprinkle the crumbled gingerbread on top. Bake for another 5 minutes until well heated through. The pears should now be completely tender and the cream thick and bubbly. Leave to cool slightly and decorate with sprigs of mint before serving straight to the table.

In the depths of winter the fruity pickings are severely depleted. I rely on pears, apples, bananas and oranges for my desserts and dried fruit asserts itself in various guises. The good thing about pears is their versatility. A ripe pear is a taste sensation. The juices dribble down your chin, and the aroma permeates your nostrils. Your fingers get sticky with the natural sugar, urging you to wash them at once lest you leave traces of the sticky nectar on everything you touch.

'Oh but', said the clever pig,
'I got a first at Trinity', before he was made into sausages.

NOVEMBER

Am I allowed, I wonder, to comment on matters other than food within the confines of this book? Oh, what the hell, it never stopped me before. I recently saw a programme called 'Grumpy Old Men', a satisfying dissertation of dissatisfaction by a group of 40-plus men on the things that most annoy them. *'That's you'*, exclaimed Máire, *'just give it another couple of years and you'll be unbearable.'*

She's right, of course. The older I get, the more crotchety I get. I'm a budding Victor Meldrew and I don't mind a bit. Permit me to tell you what irks me, along with chunky girls in belly tops; the ridiculously early appearance of Christmas decorations. In fact, more than that, the appearance of Christmas menus in late summer saying *'Book Now'* or else there may not be enough paté to go around at Christmas time.

Of course, I'm not naive. I appreciate that the unseemly glittering in November from every available window merely extols us to spend more money sooner, prematurely instilling us with Christmas spirit so when Christmas is really upon us we are almost exhausted by the fuss. Whatever happened to living for the day? There now, you have it, I can turn my attention to the food!

Actually there's one more thing, now I'm exposing some of my failings. We do frequently get asked for sample Christmas menus in August. Although I am flattered that people express an interest so soon in the year I'm left completely flummoxed. Ah, if I were only content to stick the auld turkey and ham on year after year, my life would certainly be easier but I'm afraid when the requests come I have to send them last year's menu with the assurance that it is likely to be entirely different when the time comes – call it artistic licence if you will but I admit it might seem a bit unprepared on the business front. Nothing would horrify me more than a menu sent in August or early September that might hinder me from tinkering with my menu in December.

Guinea fowl is a good option in the run up to the festive season. My reference book tells me that the guinea fowl originates in West Africa and although it is a beautiful and endearing creature, it is extremely stupid. I don't know about you but this strikes me as a little personal and just a tad cruel, for how would it matter if one animal could qualify for mensa and another was chucked out of school in baby infants as a lost cause? It seems a pretty moot point if they both end up in a pot. *'Oh but'*, said the clever pig, *'I got a first at Trinity'*, before he was made into sausages.

WHAT'S IN SEASON IN NOVEMBER

FRUIT apples, chestnuts, clementines, hazelnuts, pears, quinces and walnuts **VEGETABLES** beetroot, broccoli, brussel sprouts, cabbages, celeriac, chard, chicory, kohlrabi, leeks, lettuce, mushrooms, onions, parsnips, potatoes, pumpkins, shallots, sorrel, spinach, turnips and watercress **FISH** bass, black sole, cod, grey mullet, haddock, halibut, mackerel, mussels, oysters, red mullet and turbot **POULTRY** duck, goose, guinea fowl and turkey **GAME** hare, mallard, partridge, pheasant, pigeon, quail, rabbit, snipe, venison and woodcock.

ROASTED WINTER VEGETABLES WITH CHESTNUTS AND SPICED CRÈME FRAÎCHE

This is a robust, hearty starter that should be served warm and not hot – roasted root vegetables topped with a melting heady cream. Some smoked duck would be fab with this but I've decided to stay vegetarian for a change.

Serves 4 as a starter or light lunch

4 beetroot
1 large carrot
1 parsnip
1 small squash or turnip
4 tablespoons olive oil
1 teaspoon coriander seeds
1 teaspoon cumin seeds
200 ml / 7 fl oz crème fraîche
drizzle honey
finely grated rind 1 orange
12 pre-cooked chestnuts or some whole toasted almonds
salt and freshly ground black pepper

Preheat the oven to 200°C / 400°F / Gas 6. Wrap each beetroot in tin foil and place in a baking tin. Bake for about 1 hour until tender. Remove from the oven and leave to cool completely, then unwrap and peel away the skins. Cut each one into quarters and set aside until needed.

Cut the carrot, parsnip and squash or turnip into 2 cm / 3/4 in slices, cutting the thick parts of the parsnip and squash in half to be as similar in size as possible to the carrots. Tip them all into a roasting tin and add the olive oil, tossing to coat, then season to taste. Roast for 20 minutes, turning once or twice to ensure they all colour evenly.

Meanwhile, roast the coriander and cumin seeds in a frying pan for 1-2 minutes to bring out their flavours. Transfer to a pestle and mortar and then pound as finely as you can. Place the crème fraîche in a small serving bowl and stir in the ground spices. Cover with cling film and set aside in the fridge to allow the flavours to combine.

Remove the root vegetables from the oven, drizzle over the honey and sprinkle the orange rind on top. Toss gently until evenly coated and then cook for another 3-4 minutes or until the vegetables are completely tender and lightly caramelised.

Remove the roasted root vegetables from the oven and allow to cool for about 5 minutes, then stir in the beetroot and chestnuts or almonds and season to taste. Divide the vegetables among warmed serving bowls and place a dollop of the spiced crème fraîche on top. Serve the remaining crème fraîche on the table and allow people to help themselves.

SMOKED HADDOCK AND RAISIN CHOWDER

Everybody loves chowder. However, sometimes your expectations may be dashed with a bowl of insipid mush. This is a very simple recipe, to encourage you to make it. I love to finish it with some chopped hard-boiled egg but that's up to you. Please try to use naturally smoked haddock.

Serves 4–6 as a starter or light lunch

knob butter
100 g / 4 oz rindless streaky bacon, diced
1 large onion, chopped
4 potatoes, cut into 1 cm / $^1/_2$ in cubes
2 bay leaves
1 litre / 1$^3/_4$ pints milk
675 g / 1$^1/_2$ lb natural smoked haddock, skinned and boned
1 tablespoon raisins
2 eggs (optional – see recipe intro.)
1 bunch spring onions, trimmed and finely chopped
salt and freshly ground black pepper

Heat a large pan and add the butter. Once foaming, add the bacon and onion, then cook gently for 3-4 minutes until the onion is softened and the bacon is beginning to crisp. Add the potatoes, stirring to combine, and then pour in enough water to cover them completely. Add the bay leaves, season to taste, cover and simmer for 6-8 minutes or until the potatoes are barely tender.

Add the milk to the pan with the smoked haddock and raisins, then continue to simmer for another 15 minutes or until slightly reduced and the haddock has broken up into smaller pieces.

Meanwhile, place the eggs in a pan of water, if using, and simmer for 8-10 minutes until hard boiled, then run under the tap and crack off the shells. Chop up the hard-boiled eggs and set aside until needed.

Remove the bay leaves from the chowder and add the spring onions. Season to taste and ladle into warmed serving bowls. Scatter a little chopped hard-boiled egg over each one to serve, if you like.

TARTIFLETTE

This is a wonderful traditional French dish: an unctuous bake of potato, bacon lardons, cream and cheese. I've substituted French Reblochon for Irish Ardrahan, a jingoistic adaptation on my part. Serve this for lunch with some young spinach tossed with olive oil and sherry vinegar, or as an accompaniment to a main course.

Serves 4 as a light lunch or accompaniment

50 g / 2 oz butter
175 g / 6 oz streaky bacon, rind removed and cut into lardons
250 g / 9 oz brown mushrooms, sliced
1 kg / 2¼ lb waxy potatoes, cut into 3 mm / ⅛ in slices (use a mandolin if you've got one)
250 g / 9 oz Ardrahan cheese, cubed
550 ml / 19 fl oz cream
salt and freshly ground black pepper
dressed young spinach salad, to serve (optional – see recipe intro.)

Preheat the oven to 150°C / 300°F / Gas 2. Grease a shallow baking dish that is about 25 cm / 10 in x 30 cm / 12 in with half the butter. Heat a frying pan over a medium to high heat and add the bacon lardons.

Sauté for about 5 minutes until crisp and golden brown. Remove with a slotted spoon and drain on kitchen paper.

Return the pan to the heat and add the mushrooms to the bacon fat, then sauté for a couple of minutes until tender. Season to taste.

Season the potato slices and arrange half in an even layer in the buttered dish. Sprinkle over the bacon and mushrooms and scatter half the cheese on top. Season to taste and cover with the remaining potatoes in an attractive overlapping layer. Pour in the cream so it just covers the potatoes.

Dot the dish with the remaining butter and bake for 1 hour and 15 minutes or until the potatoes are tender. Scatter the rest of the cheese on top and return to the oven for another 5 minutes or so until brown and bubbling. Remove from the oven and allow to cool a little before serving straight on to the table with a separate bowl of spinach salad, if liked.

HONEYED QUAIL WITH LENTILS

I prefer quails on the bone. Sure, they are a little bit fiddly but eat with a finger bowl to hand and plenty of napkins and get stuck in. The lentil sauce is one I use all the time in the restaurant, either with game, meat or fish, or even on its own through some pasta it's delicious. I learned it from Shaun Hill's first book some years ago. I couldn't better it so I didn't try. This recipe could easily be served as a main course with some buttery potatoes and wilted spinach.

Serves 4 as a starter or light lunch

4 x 200 g / 7 oz quails
2 tablespoons honey
2 tablespoons soy sauce
a little sunflower oil

For the Lentils

175 g / 6 oz puy lentils
1.2 litres / 2 pints chicken stock
2 tablespoons toasted sesame oil
knob butter
1 small onion, finely diced
1 garlic clove, crushed
small knob fresh root ginger, peeled and finely diced
1 teaspoon cardamon pods, crushed and passed through a sieve
400 g / 14 oz can chopped tomatoes
2 tablespoons crème fraîche
good pinch chopped fresh coriander
squeeze fresh lemon juice
salt and freshly ground black pepper
dressed watercress and apple salad, to serve (optional)

Preheat the oven to 200°C / 400°F / Gas 6. Tuck the wings tips of the quail behind the body and tie the legs together with string. Mix the honey in a shallow non-metallic dish with the soy sauce and season to taste. Use this to coat the quails and then cover with cling film. Leave to marinate in the fridge while you make your sauce.

To make the lentils, place the lentils in a pan with the chicken stock and simmer gently for 20 minutes until the lentils are soft but still a little firm to the bite. Strain and set the lentils aside until needed.

Drain the quails from the marinade and place in a baking tin. Drizzle with the sunflower oil and bake for 20 minutes until the skin is crisp and golden brown and the meat is tender, turning them round once or twice.

To finish the lentils, heat the sesame oil in a pan and add the butter. Once it is foaming tip in the onion and then sweat for 3-4 minutes until softened and translucent. Stir in the garlic, ginger and cardamon and cook for another 3 minutes over a low heat.

Add the tomatoes to the pan and reduce by half. Tip in the cooked lentils and cook for another 2 minutes to just warm through. Stir in the crème fraîche, coriander and lemon juice and season to taste.

To serve, arrange the quails on warmed serving plates with the lentils and some of the watercress salad, if you like.

Red mullet and I go back a long way. Stunning to look at, its majestic allure mocks the drabness of other fish in our cold waters — like some South Sea island beauty that has somehow lost her way and has ruefully acclimatised yet yearns for those balmy distant shores, slashed with coral reefs, whose inhabitants dart and flitter.

BOUILLABAISSE OF MONKFISH AND MUSSELS WITH CHORIZO AND PARSNIPS

I adore seafood stews. Once you have the base sauce made all you have to do is poach your fish in it. All the flavours intermingle and sparkle. I put this one together for that and its vivid colour – I would serve this with plain boiled rice.

Serves 6–8

good splash olive oil

1 onion, chopped

2 garlic cloves, crushed

200 g / 7 oz chorizo, cut into 1 cm / $1/2$ in dice

250 ml / 9 fl oz white wine

500 ml / 16 fl oz chicken stock (a cube will do)

2 sprigs fresh rosemary

1 large parsnip, cut into 1 cm / $1/2$ in dice

300 ml / $1/2$ pint cream

600 g / 1 lb 5 oz monkfish fillet, trimmed and cut at an angle into 3 cm / $1 1/4$ in slices

2 handfuls mussels, cleaned

400 g / 14 oz can kidney beans, drained and rinsed

8 piquillo peppers, drained and diced (from a jar – optional)

$1/2$ lemon, pips removed

salt and freshly ground black pepper

plain boiled rice, to serve

Heat the oil in a large pan with a lid. Add the onion and garlic and sweat for 3-4 minutes until softened and golden. Add the chorizo and turn the heat up a little to render the oil from it. Watch that the onion mixture doesn't burn though.

Pour the wine into the pan with the stock and scrape the bottom of the pan to remove any sediment. Bring to the boil and add the rosemary and parsnip. Reduce by a quarter over a gentle heat, then add the cream and drop in the monkfish and mussels, followed by the kidney beans and piquillo peppers, if you are using them. Bring the mixture back to a gentle roll and cook for 5-6 minutes. Season to taste and add a squeeze of lemon juice. To serve, divide amongst warmed serving bowls and serve with a separate large bowl of the rice.

CORNED BEEF AND COLCANNON WITH MAPLE ROASTED CARROTS

Once September comes I reintroduce my standing order from Michael McGrath in Lismore. His corned beef is stuff of legend; all I have to do is boil it in water, removing the scum every now and then. Michael uses brisket. I find it has a very agreeable fat to meat ratio, which is essential with any cut of meat. Boil your beef earlier in the day and just reheat it in the juice when almost ready to eat. In the meantime, concentrate on your colcannon and roasting your carrots. The colcannon will be creamy enough so you won't need a sauce. A little of my apple chutney or English mustard will complete the dish.

Serves 4

1 kg / 2¼ oz corned beef (see recipe intro.)
a little sunflower oil
knob butter
3 large carrots, cut on the diagonal into 1 cm / ½ in slices
a little maple syrup

For the Colcannon

4 floury potatoes, chopped (Homeguards, Queens or Roosters)
4 large green cabbage leaves, thick stalks removed and shredded
4 spring onions, trimmed and finely chopped
good knob butter
120 ml / 4 fl oz milk
pinch freshly grated nutmeg
salt and freshly ground black pepper
apple chutney, to serve (see recipe page 179)

Place the corned beef in a large pan and cover with water. Bring to the boil, then reduce the heat and simmer for about 3 hours or until tender, occasionally skimming any scum that rises to the top. Leave to cool in the pan and then about half an hour before you are ready to serve, reheat gently.

Preheat the oven to 200°C / 400°F / Gas 6. Heat a roasting tin with the oil and butter. Add the carrots, tossing until evenly coated and season to taste. Roast for 15 minutes, turning occasionally until golden brown. Drizzle over the maple syrup and pop back in the oven for another 2 minutes until lightly caramelised.

Meanwhile, make the colcannon. Cook the potatoes in a covered pan of boiling salted water for 15-20 minutes until tender. Five minutes before the end of cooking, add the cabbage. Drain and mash the potatoes and cabbage, then beat in the spring onions, butter and milk. Season to taste and add the nutmeg, mixing well to combine.

When ready to serve, remove the string from the hot corned beef and slice against the grain. Place good dollops of the colcannon on warmed serving plates and arrange the corned beef alongside with the maple roasted carrots. Garnish with spoonfuls of apple chutney and thyme. Have an extra small dish of apple chutney on hand to pass around.

TIP

Use the leftover corned beef for sandwiches or in my corned beef croquettes, (see recipe page 146.)

I like to think I'm in touch with my feminine side.

DATE CREAM POTS WITH SPICE BISCUITS

I'm using glasses more and more with my desserts. They look good with all the swirling colours on full view and once made, they are mightily easy to serve. I ate a date and custard tart in Rockpool in Sydney last year. It was one of the nicest things I have ever eaten. Here is my homage to it.

Serves 4

50 ml / 2 fl oz milk
450 ml / 3/4 pint cream
drop vanilla extract
1 egg, plus 4 egg yolks
50 g / 2 oz caster sugar
75 g / 3 oz mascarpone cheese
2 tablespoons honey
12 soft ready-to-eat dates, cut in half to remove stones (medjool if possible)

For the Spice Biscuits

50 g / 2 oz butter
25 g / 1 oz caster sugar
75 g / 3 oz plain flour
1/2 teaspoon ground cinnamon
small pinch ground ginger

Place the milk in a pan with the cream and vanilla, then bring almost but not quite to the boil. In a separate bowl, whisk the egg, egg yolks, sugar and mascarpone cheese together.

Pour the heated milk over the egg yolk mixture and whisk well to combine. Strain through a sieve into a large bowl. Wipe out the pan and pour back in the mixture. Return to a very low heat and whisk continuously for 8-10 minutes until the mixture begins to thicken and coats the back of a wooden spoon.

Divide the dates among serving glasses and drizzle over the honey, then pour the custard mixture on top. Leave to set for 3-4 hours in the fridge or overnight is fine.

Meanwhile, make the spice biscuits. Beat the butter and sugar in a bowl until light and fluffy. Add the flour and spices and continue to beat until smooth. Bring the dough together into a ball with your hands and roll into an oval cylndrical shape that is 6cm / 1/2 in diameter, then wrap in cling film. Chill for at least an hour to firm up.

Preheat the oven to 160°C / 325°F / Gas 3. Cut the biscuit dough as thinly as possible and arrange on non-stick baking sheets. Bake for 10 minutes until lightly coloured then leave to cool for about 5 minutes before transferring on to a wire rack to cool completely.

To serve, set the glasses on serving plates and place a couple of the spice biscuits on the side of each one to serve.

CLEMENTINES IN CINNAMON CARAMEL

This is almost Christmassy in its tones. Serve these in a funky glass bowl so people can appreciate the jewel-like clementines immersed in amber nectar. Serve with crème fraîche or natural yoghurt with some toasted pecan nuts or hazelnuts, if the fancy takes you.

Serves 4

8 clementines
200 g / 7 oz sugar
2 cinnamon sticks
2 tablespoons orange-flavoured liqueur, such as Cointreau or Grand Marnier
crème fraîche and chopped toasted pecan or hazelnuts, to serve

Pare the rind from two of the clementines using a vegetable peeler and cut it into fine strips. Set aside. Peel the clementines, removing all the pith but keeping them intact, then put in a serving bowl (see recipe intro.).

Gently heat the sugar in a heavy-based pan with two tablespoons of water until the sugar melts, stirring occasionally. Increase the heat and allow to bubble until the mixture turns a rich golden colour, without stirring. Immediately turn off the heat.

Cover your hand with a tea towel and pour 300 ml / $^1/_2$ pint of warm water into the caramel - the mixture will bubble and splutter. Return to the heat and bring slowly to the boil, stirring until the caramel has dissolved. Add the reserved shredded rind and cinnamon sticks and simmer for another 5 minutes until slightly reduced. Stir in the orange-flavoured liqueur and leave the syrup to cool for about 10 minutes, then pour over the clementines and cover the bowl with a flat plate. Chill for several hours or overnight, turning occasionally so they marinate evenly.

To serve, allow the clementines to come back up to room temperature, then place the bowl straight on to the table and divide among individual serving bowls. Add dollops of crème fraîche and a sprinkling of toasted pecan or hazelnuts.

DECEMBER

Despite all my moaning in the introduction to November. I'm not a bah-humbug, Scrooge type of guy. I love Christmas. The Christmas rush doesn't bother me. In reality, it's a little bit mad coming up to Christmas Day itself. The regular parties are in attendance and are perhaps a little more boisterous than usual but that lends to the festive atmosphere in the restaurant.

The wilder crowds tend to go to the party nights in the local hotels where they can dance the night away and fight for cabs until daylight. Good luck to them. Of course, I look forward to the day itself. It can be a little stressful if I'm cooking for a crowd at home, but the effort is always worth it. Over the years my family and in-laws have become accustomed to my food obsession and have in turn become worthy and appreciative gourmands.

The week after Christmas is really my favourite. Dungarvan swells with returning emigrants, although thankfully that term seems out of place in today's Ireland. We close for lunch in between Christmas and New Year so it's a real work hard, play hard ethic. At least we can lie in if we have been bopping in the local disco the previous night.

I won't say I avoid the whole turkey and ham thing but I don't put them on the menu in a conventional way. In my last book I gave a recipe for individual ballotines of turkey and ham that I might put on but I'm a bit weary of them as the sheer volume we served last year gave me turkey phobia. Instead, I like to use smoked turkey in various ways or I might caramelise some ham and serve it with a root vegetable salad or lentils. I never really know until I see what's available. I use plenty of pheasant, goose and duck over the month, although I bear in mind that after Christmas pheasant should really be braised not roasted. If I can get goose legs that don't cost the earth I confit them and serve them with a sprout purée and an onion and chestnut gravy.

After Christmas Eve lunch, usually a crowd of friends and family call in just to chat and wish each other well. We crack open a few bottles of bubbly and talk to the children about Santa. Early to bed, be good and he will look after you. Their excitement is contagious – how could it not be? We have two days off during which I may be sponsored by Cadbury's – just as well it's back to work or those stretchy pants will be coming out. But for this short time, who cares? At home it's all about being spoilt and pampering everyone else. We take it in turns in our family to do Christmas. I have developed a bit of an aversion to leaving my house but that's hardly fair to the others. In previous years I could carouse happily late into the night and hit the sack knowing that a gentle rap on the door from my mother-in-law would wake me from my slumber. I'd wake up drowsily, bid everyone good morning, shower and go into the TV room to watch *Willy Wonka's Chocolate Factory* until Christmas lunch was ready. Granted, it was my job to carve the turkey, but this one task could get me out of the wash-up. A very good deal, I thought.

I've decided to dump my normal format for this chapter, and be utterly self indulgent. So I'll tell you about what I would like to eat on Christmas Eve, Christmas Day and St Stephen's Day. I figure that everybody is too busy to entertain in the run up to Christmas but for me there is a downside; you're finally going to see how big a gutser I really am. The recipes that follow aren't all my own. I would never be so self congratulatory to assume that it is my way or the highway.

WHAT'S IN SEASON IN DECEMBER

FRUIT apples, chestnuts, pears, pineapple, quinces and walnuts **VEGETABLES** artichokes (Jerusalem), beetroot, Brussels sprouts, cabbages, celeriac, chard, chicory, curly kale, leeks, mushrooms, onions, parsnips, salsify, turnips and watercress **FISH** bass, black sole, cod, grey mullet, haddock, halibut, mussels, oysters and turbot **POULTRY** duck, goose, guinea fowl and turkey **GAME** hare, mallard, pheasant, pigeon, rabbit, snipe, venison and woodcock.

MY CHRISTMAS MY CHRISTMAS MY CHRISTMAS MY CHRISTMA

CHRISTMAS EVE NIGHT   Baked Vacherin Mont D'Or with smoked chicken, pear and walnut salad

CHRISTMAS MORNING   Banana muffins and coffee

CHRISTMAS LUNCH   Parfait of foie gras with chicken livers and apple chutney
Duck in sweet and sour sauce with chorizo and raisin stuffing
Gratin of root vegetables
Brussels sprouts with Cidona

Iced meringue cake with hot mincemeat sauce
Chocolate truffle cake

Crozier blue with membrillo

ST STEPHEN'S DAY LUNCH   Tiger prawns with coconut and garam marsala sauce

174

VACHERIN MONT D'OR WITH SMOKED CHICKEN, PEAR AND WALNUT SALAD

Nigel Slater said it first: 'around Christmas the most voluptuous cheese known to mankind is in season.' He was talking about Vacherin Mont D'Or. It's a little hard to find admittedly but if you are lucky to have a Sheridan's cheesemongers anywhere near you they will have it, for sure. Superquinn also had a good supply last year so you can keep an eye out for it there. This cheese is baked in the oven still in its wooden casket to make the most sublime, pungent fondue you could imagine. It's normally just put on the table with some crusty bread and some tart gherkins. On my ideal Christmas Eve I could think of nothing more delicious than molten spoonfuls of this with a sharp clear salad and a chilled glass of Pineau de Charente. A simple, relaxing supper after a hectic day; enjoy with some Bing Crosby and twinkling lights.

Serves 2

1 Vacherin Mont d'Or cheese
a few walnuts (as fresh as possible – remember they're in season this month)
1 ripe pear
handful baby spinach leaves
1 smoked chicken breast, thinly sliced (I use ummera)
a little olive oil
splash sherry vinegar
salt and freshly ground black pepper
ciabatta, to serve

Preheat the oven to 200°C / 400°F / Gas 6. Wrap the cheese and its wooden casket in tin foil and bake for about 15 minutes until the skin begins to bubble and blister.

Meanwhile, place the walnuts in a small frying pan and cook for a few minutes until toasted, tossing occasionally. Remove from the heat and leave to cool.

Cut the pear into quarters and remove the core, then thinly slice and place in a bowl with the spinach and smoked chicken. Sprinkle over the olive oil and sherry vinegar, then season to taste and mix gently until nicely dressed. Divide on to serving plates as attractively as you can and scatter the toasted walnuts on top.

Remove the cheese from the oven and open up, then load it on to the serving plates beside the salad. Eat with some light ciabatta.

BANANA MUFFINS

With the day ahead of me I don't want to fill myself up with a hardcore breakfast. These muffins will tempt the soundest of sleepers from their slumber as the smell wafts around the house.

Makes 10

75 g / 3 oz butter, plus a little extra if necessary
2 large ripe bananas
250 g / 9 oz self-raising flour
1 teaspoon baking powder
pinch salt
1/2 teaspoon ground cinnamon
good pinch ground nutmeg
100 g / 4 oz caster sugar
2 eggs
few drops vanilla extract
120 ml / 4 fl oz milk
freshly brewed coffee, to serve

Preheat the oven to 190°C / 375°F / Gas 5. Melt the butter in a small pan or in the microwave and allow to cool. Peel the bananas and slice into a bowl, then mash well. Set aside until needed.

Sift the flour, baking powder, salt, cinnamon and nutmeg into a large bowl, then stir in the sugar. In a separate bowl, place the melted butter with the eggs, vanilla extract and milk, then beat until well combined. Stir in the mashed bananas.

Make a well in the centre of the dry ingredients and tip in the egg mixture, stirring roughly with a fork until it is a lumpy paste – be very careful not to over mix.

Set paper cases in a muffin tray, or grease the moulds well with a little butter and quickly spoon in the banana mixture until each mould is almost full. Bake for 20-25 minutes or until the muffins come away from the sides of the paper cases or moulds when touched.

Sit the muffin tray on a wire rack for 5 minutes, then remove the muffins and leave to cool for another 5 minutes before serving with cups of good strong coffee.

PARFAIT OF FOIE GRAS WITH CHICKEN LIVERS

This is one of my favourite creations in all the world. Unfortunately it's not mine – it's Marco Pierre White's. I also put it in my first book, such is my devotion to it. It's lighter than a regular terrine of foie gras so you won't want to lie down at the end of the meal. If you are feeling particularly decadent, decorate it with fresh figs and thyme sprigs and serve with toasted brioche and my apple chutney. If you don't fancy making the chutney, drizzle some fresh ripe figs with honey and grill for a couple of minutes. Then garnish with sprigs of thyme. If you can't get foie gras, try using 675 g / 1¹/₂ lb of chicken livers in total and you'll end up with a much lighter result.

Serves 10–12 as a starter

200 ml / 7 fl oz port
200 ml / 7 fl oz maderia
100 ml / 3¹/₂ fl oz brandy
8 shallots, thinly sliced
1 garlic clove, crushed
2 large fresh thyme sprigs
400 g / 14 oz fresh foie gras
400 g / 14 oz fresh chicken livers, well cleaned and trimmed (organic if possible)
800 g / 1 lb 10 oz unsalted butter
8 eggs (at room temperature)

To Finish

150 g / 5 oz unsalted butter
Maldon sea salt and coarsely ground white pepper
apple chutney (see page 179) and toasted brioche, to serve

Preheat the oven to 160˚C / 315˚F / Gas 2¹/₂ and have ready a non-stick terrine or paté mould that is 30 cm / 12 in x 12 cm / 4¹/₂ in and about 10 cm / 4 in deep. Place the port, maderia and brandy in a pan with the shallots, garlic and thyme, then boil fast until almost dry – you'll need about two tablespoons in total. Remove the thyme and discard.

Carefully slice the foie gras and chop the chicken livers. Place in a separate pan and cover with one tablespoon of salt. Warm gently for about 4 minutes until heated through but not coloured. Gently melt the butter in a small pan or in the microwave.
Place the reduced port mixture in a food processor or

liquidiser with the warmed livers and blend until smooth – you may need to do this in batches depending on the size of your machine. Add the eggs and blend again briefly to combine. Stir in the warm melted butter and season to taste, then working quickly push through a sieve into a bowl. Transfer to the terrine and cover tightly with a piece of tin foil.

Place the covered terrine in a bain marie (a roasting tin half filled with water) and cook for 1 hour and 10 minutes until the terrine is cooked through but still has a very slight wobble in the centre. Remove from the bain marie and leave to cool, then cover with cling film and chill for 24 hours.

To finish, melt a quarter of the butter in a small pan or in the microwave and then soften the remainder by beating it in a bowl with a wooden spoon. Slowly pour in the melted butter and using a whisk, quickly emulsify together– this lightens the butter. Spread a thin layer on top of the parfait and chill again to set.

When ready to serve, run a hot knife around the edges and turn out on to a board. If it is difficult to get out, it may be sticking on the bottom. Put a tea towel over it and pour on some boiling water. This will help loosen it.

To serve, slice the parfait with a hot knife and place a slice just below the centre of each serving plate. Sprinkle with a little sea salt and coarsely ground white pepper. Add a dollop of the apple chutney and a couple of slices of toasted brioche.

APPLE CHUTNEY

This is a beautifully intense chutney that is deep, rich and mahogany brown. It takes a long time to cook, but it keeps for ages in the fridge. Use with cheeses, cold meats and roasts over the festive season.

Makes about 2 jars

splash sunflower oil
knob butter
3 onions, finely diced
3 tablespoons Demerara sugar
250 ml / 9 fl oz red wine
100 ml / 3 ½ fl oz red wine vinegar
10 Granny Smith apples, peeled, cored and diced
1 teaspoon ground cinnamon
splash brandy

Heat the oil in a heavy-based pan with a lid, add the butter and, once foaming, add the onions and cook over a low heat for 1½ hours, stirring frequently to scrape the bottom of the pan to stop it from burning. If the onions are colouring too fast put the lid on top. When they are a nice dark brown colour, add the sugar and allow it to caramelise a little further.

Add the red wine to the pan with the red wine vinegar and bring to the boil, scraping the bottom of the pan to deglaze the sticky bits. Add the apples, cover and allow to cook for another 2 hours over a very low heat, again stirring every now and again to make sure it doesn't burn. When the 2 hours are up you should have a rich dark brown pulp. Stir in the cinnamon and brandy and leave to cool completely. Transfer to sterilised jars and chill until needed.

DUCK IN SWEET AND SOUR SAUCE WITH CHORIZO AND RAISIN STUFFING

I saw Keith Floyd cooking this dish on the telly a while ago and loved the look of it. After a little research I discovered it was an Elizabeth David recipe. I subsequently cooked it at home with this stuffing and was bowled over.

Serves 8

50 g / 2 oz butter
a little sunflower oil
2 large onions, thinly sliced
pinch ground cloves
2 x 1.8-2.25 kg / 4-5 lb oven-ready ducks
400 ml / 14 fl oz chicken stock
2 tablespoons sugar
2 tablespoons red wine vinegar

For the Chorizo and Raisin Stuffing

small handful raisins
small handful almonds
100 g / 4 oz butter
1 small onion, finely chopped
splash olive oil
150 g / 5 oz chorizo, finely diced
2 tablespoons chopped fresh flat-leaf parsley
finely grated rind of 1 orange
225 g / 8 oz fresh white breadcrumbs
salt and freshly ground black pepper
gratin of roasted vegetables and Brussels sprouts with Cidona, to serve (optional – see recipes page 184 and 185)

Preheat the oven to 180°C / 350°F / Gas 5. To make the stuffing, soak the raisins in a bowl of boiling water for twenty minutes, then drain. Toast the almonds in a small frying pan for a few minutes, tossing occasionally so they colour evenly. Melt the butter in a pan and gently sauté the onion for 3-4 minutes until softened but not coloured. Tip into a large bowl. Heat the olive oil in a frying pan and sauté the chorizo for two minutes until the colour starts to bleed. Add to the onion with the soaked raisins, toasted almonds, parsley, orange rind and bread-crumbs. Season to taste and mix lightly to combine but not too much or it will go pasty. Use to stuff the ducks, but do not jam pack the cavities, and secure with cocktail sticks.

Heat a heavy-based large ovenproof pan or oval casserole dish with a lid, big enough to take both ducks and use to melt the butter and sunflower oil. Season each duck and add to the pan. Cook until nicely coloured all over, then remove from the pan and set aside on a large plate. Reduce the pan's heat right down and add the onions. Cook for about 10 minutes or until completely softened and golden, scraping the bottom of the pan occasionally to remove any sediment. Stir in the cloves and return the ducks to the pan, then pour over the stock. Cover and transfer to the oven for 1 ½ hours. Remove the lid from the pan and cook for another 30 minutes to allow the ducks to caramelise, basting every now and then. When the ducks are completely tender and the skins are crispy, remove them from the pan and keep them warm in a low pre-heated oven.

Pour off as much fat as possible from the sauce. In a separate small pan, heat the sugar with two table-spoons of water, until the sugar has dissolved, then increase the heat and boil fast until caramel in colour, without stirring. Stir into the sauce with the vinegar and season to taste, then continue to simmer for a

few minutes until the sauce is thickened with a syrup-like consistency. Pour into a warmed gravy boat and keep warm.

To serve, carve the ducks into slices and arrange on warmed serving plates with a spoonful of the chorizo and raisin stuffing. Add some of the gratin of root vegetables and Brussels sprouts with Cidona, if you like. Pass around the sauce separately and allow people to help themselves.

GRATIN OF ROOT VEGETABLES

This is everything I love baked together to make one of the most delicious things you will ever taste. Use a mandolin if you have one to slice the vegetables. It will make life a great deal easier.

Serves 8

25 g / 1 oz butter
400 g / 14 oz parsnips, thinly sliced
400 g / 14 oz turnips, thinly sliced
400 g / 14 oz potatoes, thinly sliced
900 ml / 1 ^{1}/$_2$ pints cream
300 ml / ^{1}/$_2$ pint milk, plus a little extra if necessary
2 garlic cloves, crushed
a little chopped fresh thyme
salt and freshly ground black pepper

Preheat the oven to 180°C / 350°F / Gas 4. Butter a large ovenproof dish. Place the parsnips, turnips and potatoes in a large bowl and season well. Pour the cream and milk into a pan and add the garlic, then bring to the boil. Remove from the heat.

Arrange one-third of the vegetables in the bottom of the buttered dish and cover with one-third of the cream mixture, then sprinkle a little of the thyme over. Repeat this twice, pressing the final layer of vegetables down with a fish slice so they are submerged beneath the cream mixture. If it seems a little dry, top up with a little more milk.

Bake the gratin for 45-50 minutes, pressing down the vegetables again after 15 minutes. It is ready when the vegetables are completely tender and the top is golden and crusty. Serve straight on to the table and allow people to help themselves.

BRUSSELS SPROUTS WITH CIDONA

You might think this recipe is a bit mad. However, we used to drink Cidona with our Christmas dinner! it was not just the kids who drank it, mind you, but my parents too. Not for them the Black towers, Blue nuns and Mateus Rosés of the time. Regular wine drinkers inhabited the leafy suburbs of Dublin, a place we so rarely visited. It might well have been Kazakhstan. There was a shop to tend to six days a week all through the year and one Sunday a month in rotation with the other chemists in town. Anyhow, I've always liked sprouts, and as it goes you take a bite of sprout, slosh it around in the gravy, pop it into your mouth, chew a little (albeit less than I should for I was very keen to get at the rest of the dinner) then take a gulp of Cidona. The sweetness of the drink would balance the bitterness of the sprout thereby making it child friendly. With this in mind some years later I tried this little number. Now it's a regular fixture in the Flynn household at Christmas.

Serves 8

675 g / 1½ lb Brussels sprouts, trimmed
50 g / 2 oz butter
300 ml / ½ pint bottle Cidona (carbonated apple drink)
salt and freshly ground black pepper

Place the Brussels sprouts in a pan of boiling salted water and bring to the boil, then reduce the heat and simmer gently for 5 minutes until just tender. Drain and quickly refresh under cold running water. Place in a bowl and cover with cling film until needed – this can be done up to 24 hours in advance.

Heat a sauté pan and add the butter. Once foaming, tip in the blanched Brussels sprouts and sauté on a medium heat, turning every now and again until they start to lightly brown. Pour in the Cidona, increase the heat and simmer until all the liquid has absorbed into the sprouts, shaking the pan a couple of times. Season to taste and tip into a warmed serving bowl to serve.

TIP

If you can't find Cidona use 7-Up!

ICED MERINGUE CAKE WITH HOT MINCEMEAT SAUCE

You will have figured my obsession with meringue by now. This is not, strictly speaking, an ice cream, but meringues and cream mixed together and frozen in a pudding mould. It's light and easy. The mincemeat sauce is a revelation. Nothing like the gooey mixtures we are used to. Laced with a little rum, it anoints the cold cream and they melt into one another delightfully.

Serves 8

a little rapeseed or sunflower oil
500 ml / 16 fl oz cream
1 tablespoon sieved icing sugar
2 drops vanilla extract or even better the scraped seeds from 1 vanilla pod
8 meringue shells (shop-bought or homemade)

For the Hot Mincemeat Sauce

good knob butter
1 tablespoon Demerara sugar
finely grated rind and juice of 1 orange
2 Granny Smith apples, peeled, cored and cut into 1 cm / 1/2 in dice
2 slightly firm bananas, peeled and cut into 1 cm / 1/2 in dice
handful pecan nuts, halved lengthways
1 tablespoon raisins
pinch ground cinnamon
splash dark rum

Have a 900 ml / 1 1/2 pint plastic pudding basin or similar sized ceramic bowl at the ready and lightly oil. Whip the cream in a large bowl until soft peaks form, then fold in the icing sugar and vanilla. Break each meringue shell roughly into three pieces and add to he bowl. Stir just enough to mix. Fill the pudding basin with the meringue mixture up to the brim. Cover with cling film or a lid and freeze overnight.

To make the hot mincemeat sauce, melt the butter in a frying pan and add the sugar. Cook a little over a medium heat until it just starts to caramelise, then stir in the orange juice. Add the apples, bananas, pecan nuts, raisins and cinnamon with the orange rind. Cook for 4–5 minutes until everything starts to soften and amalgamate, stirring occasionally. Pour in the rum and allow the sauce to boil for another few seconds. Remove from the heat and allow to cool. Transfer to a bowl and cover with cling film, then place in the fridge until needed. This can happily be made up to 24 hours in advance.

To prepare the cake, you'll need to turn it out before you start to eat and put it back into the freezer. Simply run a knife along the edge of the bowl and then sit into a larger bowl of hot water for a few seconds. Place a flat plate on top and invert. To serve, reheat the sauce in a pan. Slice the iced meringue cake into wedges and arrange on serving plates. Spoon the hot mincemeat sauce on the side to serve.

CHOCOLATE TRUFFLE CAKE

I'm not necessarily going to make two desserts on the day but I wanted to give you a choice. My plan is to have the ice cream cake and scoff my body weight in Skelligs chocolates in front of the telly later.

Serves 10–12

400 g / 14 oz unsalted butter
200 g / 7 oz cocoa powder
200 g / 7 oz plain chocolate (at least 55 per cent cocoa solids)
600 ml / 1 pint cream
75 g / 3 oz icing sugar, sifted
10 egg yolks
350 g / 12 oz caster sugar

For the Biscuit Base

75 g / 3 oz butter
275 g / 10 oz digestive biscuits

To make the biscuit base, melt the butter in a small pan or in the microwave. Crush the biscuits in a food processor or in a polythene bag with a rolling pin, then tip into a bowl. Stir in the melted butter until well combined and then press into a 25 cm / 10 in springform cake tin. Place in the fridge for 20 minutes to set.

To make the cake mixture, place the unsalted butter and cocoa powder in a heatproof bowl set over a pan of simmering water for a few minutes until the butter has melted and the cocoa powder has dissolved, stirring occasionally. Remove from the heat and then melt the chocolate in a separate bowl. Stir the melted chocolate into the butter mixture and set aside to cool a little.

Place the cream and icing sugar in a large bowl and whip to a thick ribbon stage. Whisk the egg yolks and caster sugar in another bowl until thick and creamy, then fold in the chocolate mixture. Finally fold in the whipped sweetened cream until you have achieved an even consistency and colour.

Carefully pour the cake mixture over the set biscuit base and smooth over the top. Chill for at least 3 hours or overnight is best, especially if you have a full fridge. Cut into slices with a hot knife for nice sharp edges and arrange on serving plates to serve.

This would be fantastic served with some prunes. soaked in Armagnac.

CROZIER BLUE WITH MEMBRILLO

Crozier blue is made by the same people that make Cashel Blue. It's a delicate sheep's cheese, soft and luscious and when eaten with membrillo, that famous quince jam from Spain, and some oatcakes makes me delirious with pleasure. A fine glass of port completes the experience; I couldn't finish a special meal any other way.

TIGER PRAWNS WITH COCONUT AND GARAM MASALA SAUCE

I thought long and hard about this dish, after the previous days gorge-fest. I wanted a change of tack, some new flavours to taste. This sauce is fabulous, and I could put it with meat. The trouble is I wanted to eat fish on St Stephen's Day. I had envisaged a lively tray of mixed seafood covered with this sauce and baked. It couldn't be easier except where do you find fish on St Stephen's Day unless you go out and catch it yourself? It was looking like a no go. I thought freezing was out of the question or was it? Tiger prawns tails are readily available before Christmas imported from the Far East. These babies are still stupendous, despite being frozen. So make your sauce, then poach your prawns in the sauce along with some peas and cashew nuts – both from packets so there is very little work. You'll probably need to make a trip to the Asia market on Dury Street in Dublin or a similar establishment elsewhere in the country to get some of the more unusual ingredients but the results are well worth the effort. Serve with either boiled or pilaff rice (see recipe page 31) and fresh chopped coriander.

Serves 8

350 g / 12 oz basmati or Thai fragrant rice
40-50 frozen tiger prawns, thawed and shells removed
225 g / 8 oz frozen petit pois
100 g / 4 oz roasted salted cashew nuts

For the Sauce

splash sunflower oil
1 small onion, finely diced
3 green chillies, sliced (remove the seeds if you don't like things too hot)
1 large garlic clove, finely chopped
1 teaspoon ground turmeric
175 g / 6 oz tomato purée
350 ml / 12 fl oz chicken stock
2 x 400 g / 14 oz cans coconut milk
3 kaffir lime leaves (fresh, frozen or dried)
knob fresh root ginger, peeled and grated
2 tablespoons Thai fish sauce (*nam pla*)
50 g / 2 oz palm sugar
2 teaspoons garam masala
salt and freshly ground black pepper
chopped fresh coriander, to garnish

To make the sauce, place the oil in a large pan and add the onion, chillies and garlic, then cook for a few minutes until golden, stirring occasionally. Stir in the turmeric and tomato purée and allow to heat through, then add the chicken stock, coconut milk, lime leaves, ginger, fish sauce, palm sugar and garam marsala. Bring to the boil, then reduce the heat and simmer for 5 minutes until slightly reduced and thickened. Allow to cool a little, then ladle into a food processor or liquidiser and blend until smooth – you may have to do this in batches. Pass through a sieve into a bowl. Cover with cling film and chill until needed.

When ready to serve, cook the rice in a pan of boiling salted water for 10-12 minutes until tender or according to the packet instructions. Tip the coconut and garam marsala sauce into a pan and reheat gently. Season the prawns and add to the pan, then poach for 3 minutes. Add the peas and cook for another 2 minutes. Add the cashew nuts and allow to warm through. Drain the rice and divide among warmed serving plates, then spoon the tiger prawn curry over. Scatter the coriander on top and serve at once.

INDEX OF RECIPES

MAY

Asparagus with Creamy Goats' Cheese, Apple and Mint Dressing 67
Asian Lamb Salad 68
Potato Cakes with Smoked Mackerel, Mango and Cucumber Dressing 69
Roast Belly of Pork, Beetroot Tsatziki and Rocket 71
Peppered Duck Breast, Glazed Red Onions and Champ 72
Roasted Monkfish, Braised Lettuce, Tarragon and Red Onion Cream 74
Gooseberry Crisp 76
Chocolate Ripple Semifreddo with Amaretto Caramel 78

JUNE

Summer Vegetable Broth with Herby Dumplings 82
Spring Onion Omelette with Gravadlax and Mustard Dressing 84
Crab Toes with Rocket, Lemon and Ginger 85
Chorizo, New Potato, Egg and Little Gem Salad 87
Courgette Risotto with Knockalara Cheese, Tomato and Basil 88
Baked Seafood with Pernod Cream, Penne, Fennel and Sunblush Tomatoes 90
Strawberry Yoghurt Meringues 92
Custard Tart with Poached Rhubarb and Ginger 95

JULY

Pappa Al Pomodoro with Prawns, Tomato and Bread Soup 100
Knockalara Cheese with Fresh Peaches, French Beans and Olives 101
Summer Vegetable and Potato Salad 102
Grilled Lambs' Liver with Cumin, Apricots and Tabbouleh 103
Rib Eye Steak and Soft Polenta, with Spring Onions and Desmond Cheese 105
Butter-poached Wild Salmon, with Parsley Crushed Potatoes 106
Sweet and Sour Mackerel with Carrots, Red Onion and Chickpeas 108
Cherry Summer Pudding with White Chocolate Flakes 109

AUGUST

Marinated Cherry Tomato Salad with Boilie Cheese 113
Watermelon Gazpacho 115
Smoked Chicken, Pasta Salad with Peas and Cashew Nuts 116
Oriental Crab Risotto 117
Lamb Chops with Mustard and Caper Butter 118
Baked Black Pollock with Tomatoes, Olives and Garlic 120
Summer Berry Trifle 122
Cherry Berries 125

INDEX